12/3

BROOCHES

BROOCHES

TIMELESS ADORNMENT

Lori Ettlinger Gross

photography by David Behl

RIZZOLI
NEW YORK

First published in the United States of America in 2008
by Rizzoli International Publications, Inc.
300 Park Avenue South
New York, New York 10010
www.rizzoliusa.com

Fabrics courtesy of Old World Weavers/Stark Fabric: Front cover, pages 3, 6, 65, 85, 89, 148
Quadrille Wallpapers and Fabrics, Inc., China Seas, and Quadrille Couture: pages 2, 13, 14-15, 16, 25, 44-45,
46, 67, 69, 72-73,74, 87, 90, 93, 98, 101, 103, 104, 120-121, 124, 127, 138-139, 140, 144, 155, 162, 167, 176-177, 180

2008 2009 2010 2011 / 10 9 8 7 6 5 4 3 2 1

Printed in China

ISBN: 0-8478-3143-4
ISBN 13: 978-0-8478-3143-2

Library of Congress Control Number: 2007942630

Project Editor: Sandra Gilbert
Designers: Miko McGinty, Doug Clouse, and Rita Jules

Pages 2: A 1940s diamond, ruby, and platinum bow brooch is a wonderful foil
to a jacket in a luxurious print. Courtesy of Olivia Collings Antiques; 5: Cranberry pin. Hand-patinaed
bronze with colored freshwater pearls; 2007. Courtesy of Silver Seasons;
6: Platinum, sapphires, and natural yellow diamond brooch. French, circa 1935.
This piece is an example of "nail-head" setting, and every sapphire is individually cut to
fit the mounting. Courtesy of The DeYoung Collection.

For Larry, Joshua, Joel, and Jarett

– with all my love.

Introduction
The Brooch: From Daily Essential to Enduring Jewel
8

Chapter 1: HISTORY
14

Chapter 2: CRAFT
44

Chapter 3: COLLECTING
72

Chapter 4: STYLE
120

Chapter 5: PIN-OLOGY
138

Chapter 6: CARE
178

Addresses
188

Acknowledgments
190

THE BROOCH

FROM DAILY ESSENTIAL TO ENDURING JEWEL

A brooch is a powerful object. Within the confines of a relatively small composition, it is a complete work of art. Each one has a voice; some have personal meaning, others have artistic merit, and a few have both. I once met a woman who was wearing a beautiful art deco brooch. I complimented her, expressing my admiration, and she thanked me graciously. Her smile remained sociable, but guarded. When I then explained my background as a jewelry historian, her expression relaxed and she bloomed with enthusiasm. The brooch was an anniversary gift from her husband. It symbolized the many hours they spent together visiting museums and sifting through flea market stalls. It embodied their shared passion for collecting.

A smattering of silver pins is a natural addition to a jean jacket. Mixing rhinestone pieces with metal-intensive ones offers a nice balance of glitter and gleam. Shell, leaf, grapes, and acorn brooches, Collection of Pam Sommers. All others, author's collection.

Mogul-influenced Cartier art deco clip/brooch set in platinum and mounted with jade, enamel, sapphires, rubies, and diamonds; circa 1925. Private collection, courtesy of Williams Galleries, Nashville.

For me, this example possessed classic art deco elements that made the period so intoxicating and eternally chic. Produced by Cartier during the 1920s, the brooch was a confluence of modern geometries sculpted in platinum, diamonds, sapphires, emeralds, and a simple slice of jadeite. The piece was made when the blending of exotic cultures, architecture, and modern art filtered through the jewelry trade producing refined designs that to this day remain quintessentially urbane. This period also brought together Cartier and art deco; these words together hold significant meaning to the jewelry cognoscenti who appreciate the era for its fine artisanship and innovative design.

A brooch doesn't have to be a collector-worthy masterpiece in order to be fabulous. It can also be a simple affair. Pins and brooches originally were practical devices. The word brooch comes from the French word *broche*, which means "skewer" or "long needle"; the word pin comes from the old English "pinn," which means "peg" or "bolt." The pin on the back of a brooch is a device that allows the wearer to secure the ornament to a woven or knitted surface that will support it. Many people think of smaller pieces as pins and view larger, more impressive forms as brooches. Family tradition—how your mother or grandmother referred to them—largely determines whether you use the word pin or brooch. In the 1930s, a "clip" commonly referred to a brooch worn at the neckline of a dress; the pin mechanism at the back of the ornament could both pierce the fabric and snap down onto the garment. Jewelers still use this expression today. It does not matter if the jewel is called a pin, brooch, or clip as these labels are now used interchangeably.

Their mercurial nature keeps us captivated because there is always a different perspective to explore. What else works with an asymmetrical neckline or can be worn on a belt, bag, or shoe? Why does a jean jacket suddenly become a standout when it's adorned with flash and glitter? A sexy little black suit gains a shot of Victorian opulence with a floral spray of nineteenth-century diamonds pinned to one shoulder. Only a brooch could dramatically alter the look of this ensemble because it creates an immediate impact without interfering with the silhouette of the dress. Earrings are wonderful but their sole aim is to frame and complement a woman's face. Because a pin is affixed to cloth, it affects the overall perception of the garment as well as the woman wearing it.

That persistent question we ask ourselves while standing in front of a mirror, "Does this look good on me?," just doesn't apply to brooches. They look good on everyone. It's always the sum total that counts. Pins are not like earrings where size, metal color, or shape must be considered. Pins are self-contained works of art, attached to a surface that will support them. Simply adding a brooch to the lapel of a basic navy blue blazer or placing a clip to the waistline of a skirt immediately transforms the look. Once pinned on, the magic it works is all its own.

The way a brooch is worn is a form of personal expression. Throwing a few scatter pins on a collar or turtleneck adds a dash of sophistication to a closet staple. A pin draws attention to wherever you position it, so slipping one in your hair brings attention to your face in an understated, alluring way. Patron of the Harkness Ballet, Rebecca Harkness, was photographed chicly dressed and bejeweled in a couture gown with her Salvador Dalí *Etoile de Mer* (starfish) brooch draped squarely over her left breast. Surrealism is often about unexpected juxtapositions.

Once you begin to notice the ways people wear this type of jewelry, you realize they possess a universal appeal that defies gender and age. Women in all stages of life enjoy brooches. Men wear them too. Some don small pins like a flag or an emblem of political affiliation. Others actually embrace the pin as a dapper, man-about-town accessory; one jeweler I know wears a stickpin in the form of a racing jockey, carved in luminous moonstone, on his bespoke suit jacket. A pin may be relatively small in size but it projects a significant message about personal style.

Art deco floral pin by Lacloche. Mounted in diamonds, sapphires, pink sapphires, emeralds, and citrine. France, circa 1930. Courtesy of Siegelson New York.

Diamond and demantoid (green) garnet butterfly pin mounted in gold; circa 1890. Courtesy of Frances Klein.

Diamond and emerald clip. Mounted in platinum and set with diamonds and emerald; circa 1930. Courtesy of Frances Klein.

Emerald and diamond clips by Paul Flato. Mounted in platinum and set with emeralds and diamonds; circa 1935. Private collection. Jeweler to Hollywood movie stars of the 1930s, Flato created some of the most original jewels of the period.

There is no limit to how you can express yourself with pins and brooches because they come in endless variations, from fine to costume. They are made from every type of material and have long been considered prime examples of the art of the goldsmith, enamelist, stone setter, artisan, or designer. Many illustrations of pins and brooches are provided throughout this book; each one has a singular appeal and was chosen for its distinctive style, motif, color palette, or extraordinary composition. Decorative time periods covering more than two hundred years, from the late eighteenth to the twenty-first centuries, are represented throughout, unequivocally demonstrating how these practical ornaments have evolved into incredibly desirable and fashionable objects. Yet this accounts for only part of the story; an interesting brooch or pin also demands clever placement. Often an outfit becomes spectacular simply with the addition of a well-located brooch.

This unique form of jeweled adornment requires little more than a few millimeters of fabric upon which to perch. What the jewel looks like should matter primarily to the wearer. A Victorian gold and diamond masterpiece can be worn with the same élan as a beautifully engraved high-school graduation medal from 1918. Wear a brooch to express your individuality or to boast your point of view. These ornaments have embellished everything from togas to ball gowns, and blazers to jean jackets, remaining fashionable across the span of centuries—thus proving the brooch is truly a timeless adornment.

Chapter 1

HISTORY

*P*INS were born of necessity. Initially crafted from finely honed flint, they were used in the Neolithic Age when cave dwellers sought protection from the elements by fastening animal skins together.

As early as 2500 B.C., evidence of jewelry was found in what was once the Sumerian city of Ur, today southern Iraq. The dress-pin, the first ancestor to our present-day version, was a functional item used to attach clothing in the same way we now rely on buttons or snaps. It was long and slender and had a decorative element at the top, such as a sculptural detail or primitively cut gems. Over the centuries, pins evolved from practical items to elaborate jewels desired for their beauty. Fashion has played an essential role in altering this perspective. The pin has always been able to complement ever-changing clothing trends without losing its relevance.

Cut-steel rosette brooch. Antique brooches have a way of eliciting an evocative response when pinned to a contemporary jacket. This ornament, circa 1850, was part of a *demi-parure*, or suite of jewels, that includes matching earrings. The gemlike elements were created by faceting tiny pieces of steel and then riveting each one by hand through a steel plate. This laborious process produced jewelry that sparkled brilliantly and simulated the look of diamonds. Courtesy of Olivia Collings Antiques.

AN ILLUSTRATED CHRONOLOGY

 *T*HE timeline that follows illustrates significant developments in the history of the brooch. It is not an exhaustive list of all brooches created or every technological advance in their manufacture. This chronological account is provided as a useful reference to understand how fashion, technological ingenuity, and artistry shaped the evolution of pins and brooches and reinforced their place as personal adornments.

Brooches can work almost anywhere: on the shoulder, the waistline of a skirt, or even on a cloche. Capucine wears a black Jean Barthet fur cap embellished with a row of diamond "Flame" clips, created in 1934 by Van Cleef & Arpels.
Photograph © D. R.; courtesy of Van Cleef & Arpels.

Fibula

Technology in metalwork progressed rapidly during the late Bronze Age in northwestern Europe. Wire was bent, coiled, and twisted into decorative forms. Early examples of fibulae had no catch and were simply threaded twice through the garment, then secured by bending the pin and latching it behind the head of the ornament. They secured Roman tunics and were said to be used to close the veils of the Vestal Virgins. Later fibulae took on the more familiar look of a safety pin, a nineteenth-century innovation.

This reproduction of an ancient fibula was used in the Emmy-award-winning HBO series, *Rome*. The design, selected by costume designer April Ferry, was crafted by the show's metalsmith, Luca Giampaoli. Courtesy of HBO.

Ring Brooch

One of the most common medieval jewels worn
during the thirteenth century, the ring brooch was
most often used to close the neckline of a dress.
They were circular in form, and many had personal
inscriptions known as posies. One example from
Writtle, England, stated plainly, "I am a brooch to
guard the breast that no rascal may put his hand
thereon." This ornament fell completely out of favor
by 1500 when necklines plunged and décolletage
became fashionable again.

Hat Badge or Enseigne

Worn on a man's hat or cap, this sixteenth-century ornament indicated political or social prominence. England's King Henry VIII wore numerous examples, which can be seen in his portraits. Hat badges were often decorated with mythological or biblical motifs, portraits, a monogram, or the image of a patron saint. They were usually made of gold but have been found in copper and bronze and pinned or sewn to the underside of an upturned brim of a hat. Women added them to their fashionable headgear from the mid-sixteenth until the early seventeenth century, when they were replaced by the feathery and more flattering aigrette (see page 26).

Aglet

A small pin-like and bejeweled item, the aglet was used as a decorative element on clothing from the sixteenth to the seventeenth centuries. Queen Elizabeth I ordered dresses with hundreds of pearl aglets floating across the deep folds of her skirts and holding together the dozens of tiny pleats that highlighted her sleeves. Pearls were viewed as highly valuable—more so than diamonds—because they were found in oysters in the ocean's depths and could only be hand-collected by divers who faced innumerable dangers. The magnificent and large pearls viewed in so many contemporary portraits of the queen were of the very best quality, making them even more rare. Each and every aglet was sewn to her majesty's clothing by hand and later removed, only to be re-attached to another voluminous garment. No doubt there weren't many pin enthusiasts among her diligent but weary tailors and seamstresses.

·ANNO·ETATIS· ·SVÆ·XLIX·

Sévigné or Ribbon Bow Brooch

Ribbon bow brooch mounted in gold and set with diamonds and emeralds; nineteenth century. Courtesy of Fred Leighton.

This flirtatious ornament was named after the Marquise de Sévigné, a member of Louis XIV's court and renowned for her eloquent letter writing. The ribbon bow brooch was considered de rigueur for any eighteenth-century woman, especially one who had to navigate the sometimes perilous waters of court life. How these pins were worn signaled more than good taste. A silent lexicon called "ribbon language" offered a choice of messages: If a bow was worn over the heart, this indicated that the wearer had found true love; a bow dangling around the neck and precipitously over the heart said "perhaps"; and one worn over the décolletage was an unambiguous invitation for intimate contact. The brooch usually was set entirely with diamonds and had additional diamonds or pearls hanging from its framework.

Aigrette

Taking its name and shape from the egret's plume, this type of brooch was worn in the hair or attached to a diadem. Aigrettes were gem-laden and glamorous and sometimes featured actual feathers. More elaborate versions were set *en tremblant* (trembling), where silver or gold stalks of wheat or feathers were mounted with diamonds and set on springs or coiled wires that gently swayed in the breeze as the wearer glided across the dance floor. Under candlelight, the effect of glittering gems filling the dimmed void of a ballroom must have been spectacular. Fashionable during the seventeenth and eighteenth centuries, the aigrette again resurfaced during the nineteenth and early twentieth centuries.

A rose-cut diamond cluster surmounted by a graduated diamond spray. Set in silver and gold with a later brooch fitting; circa 1810. Courtesy of Christies.

Portrait Miniature

A Georgian miniature of Cupid sailing on his quiver. Hand-painted on ivory and mounted in a gold frame; circa 1820. Courtesy of Kentshire Galleries, Ltd.

During the eighteenth century, well before the age of photography, wealthy patrons commissioned small painted portraits that were mounted in gold or silver frames; some were set with precious stones and pearls. This jewel was worn as a pin-pendant. The subject matter varied and included Greek mythological figures.

Starburst brooch mounted in platinum-topped-gold and set with diamonds; circa 1910. Crescent-shaped man-in-the-moon pin mounted in gold and set with diamonds and pearls; circa 1880. Both are courtesy of Kentshire Galleries, Ltd.

Sunburst and Crescent Brooches

Celestial representations and their mystical beauty were favored from the eighteenth to the early twentieth centuries, especially after the appearance of Halley's Comet in 1758 and in 1835. Heavenly examples of the eighteenth century were commonly mounted in diamonds that were foiled to optimize their brilliance and then mounted in closed-back settings. By the early nineteenth century, stone-cutting technology had improved, and diamonds were mounted in open-back settings—a technique called *ajoure* work, which permitted the maximum amount of light to penetrate the bottom and sides of the gemstone, thus giving it more sparkle.

Stomacher or bodice ornament. White pastes imitating rose-cut diamonds set in silver. Probably England; circa 1720. Courtesy of V&A Images/Victoria and Albert Museum.

Stomacher

This jewel, also known as a bodice ornament, was pinned to the triangular section beneath the bust-line and worn from the décolletage to below the waist. Heavily gem-set in ribbon or floral motifs, these majestic jewels were often made in sections, enabling the individual elements to be detached and used separately. This ornament was fashionable in the seventeenth and eighteenth centuries; its popularity revived during the Edwardian period in the early twentieth century.

Mourning Pin

Worn by bereaved family members in the eighteenth century and into the early part of the nineteenth, these pins often contained a receptacle for hair and were inscribed with the name of the deceased and the birth and death dates. They were set with small gems and pearls, which represented tears. Mourning pins took many forms, including ones made from the hair of the deceased. After the death of Prince Albert in 1861, Queen Victoria made the mourning pin an essential part of everyday attire. The strictest period of mourning was observed by wearing brooches set with jet or a black glass substitute known as French jet.

French jet mourning pin; circa 1900. Author's collection.

Jabot Pin

This pin was inserted into a necktie or scarf and sported a matching or coordinating decorative element at either end of the ornament. Popular during the art deco period, it was frequently worn on a hat or suit lapel.

Stickpin

Also known as a tie or cravat pin, the stickpin was secured to a necktie or scarf. The top of the pin always supports a decorative element that can be figural or gem set, occasionally both. Similar to the stickpin is the hat pin. Long and slender, these pins were used to keep a woman's hat in place. Usage began during the mid-nineteenth century and lasted until almost 1940. Hat pins could be simple or elaborately decorated with gems or other ornamentation such as blown glass, ivory, jet, or tortoiseshell.

Silver-topped-gold jabot pin. Set with diamonds and emeralds; nineteenth century. Courtesy of Fred Leighton.

These Miriam Haskell stickpins are set with glass pearls and white rhinestones. Courtesy of The RSL Collection.

Florentine Mosaic and Micromosaic Brooches

Taking the Grand Tour in the latter part of the nineteenth century was an indication of one's cultural sophistication. In Italy, tourists bought these small souvenirs as jeweled mementos. Florentine or hard-stone mosaics were made from semiprecious gems and their designs depicted flora and fauna. As popular during the time as cameos, Roman mosaics were pictorial compositions resembling a jigsaw puzzle created entirely of minute shards of glass called tesserae. Subjects included ancient Roman architecture, landscapes, flowers, animals, and birds.

A nineteenth-century *pietra dura* (hardstone) brooch. The rectangular panel depicts a parrot and butterfly, and is set with gemstones including lapis lazuli and malachite, within an oval gold surround stamped with scrolls and with applied textured flowerheads. Courtesy of Christies.

Micromosaic. Mounted in gold and set with glass tesserae; nineteenth century. Courtesy of Fred Leighton.

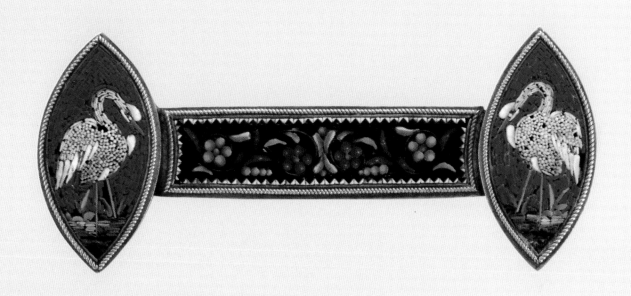

Bar Brooch

Gold Etruscan-revival bar brooch with sun and moon masks; circa 1870. Courtesy of Kentshire Galleries, Ltd.

Long and horizontal, these brooches debuted in the 1890s. They were commonly worn in groupings, which gave them a more impressive appearance. They could be gem set, engraved, enameled, or elaborately worked with granulation.

Lace Pin

Flower lace pin mounted in gold, decorated in enamel, and set with a diamond; circa 1900. Courtesy of The DeYoung Collection.

Also known as a *fichu* pin, this brooch was used to secure the delicate woven scarves women wore around their shoulders during the eighteenth and early nineteenth centuries. Later versions were smaller and worn in multiples, like scatter pins. They remained popular well into the twentieth century.

Bouquet brooch by Verdura. Mounted in platinum and set with heart-shaped amethyst, turquoise, and diamonds; circa 1949. Courtesy of Newcal Galleries, Ltd.

These clever diamond and platinum dress clips by Yaeche Freres come with a brooch mounting that locks the two pieces together so that they can be worn as a single unit. When separated, the pair may be converted for use as earrings. French; circa 1935. Courtesy of James Robinson, Inc.

Floral Brooch

This was the centerpiece of a woman's jewelry wardrobe throughout the eighteenth and nineteenth centuries. Many were styled as large corsage ornaments to be worn on the bodice of an evening gown. From the twentieth century to the present time, floral brooches remain a much loved motif.

Dress Clip

These ornaments originated during the 1930s and 1940s and were the most versatile of jewelry items. They could be worn in pairs at the corners of a neckline, on a belt, or pinned to an evening bag or sash. Others served as decorative elements of a bracelet or *minaudiere* (evening bag) that could be removed and worn separately.

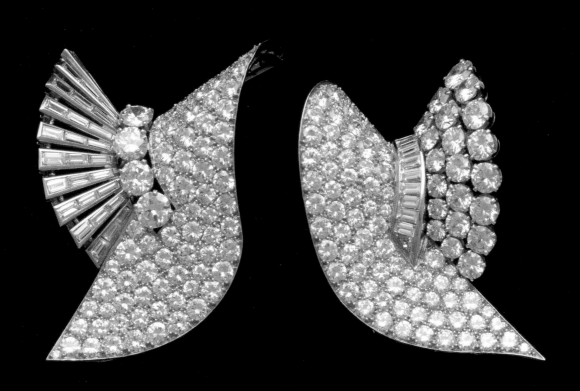

Flowerpot Brooch

This is pin style that manifested itself in several forms over the centuries. In the 1700s it was known as *giardinetti*, the Italian term for garden; small gems represented each bloom. This style continued into the nineteenth century. It evolved in the twentieth century becoming finely detailed, gem-laden ornaments as well as less costly, yet very attractive costume jewelry. In the mid-1920s, the stylized flowerpot brooch mounted in platinum, diamonds, and carved precious gems became a classic jewel of the art deco period.

Lapel Watch

Worn on the lapel of a jacket or coat, these pins were the height of style and practicality during the 1920s and 1930s.

....

Platinum and enamel art deco pendant watch set with rubies, sapphires, emeralds, and diamonds. Signed "Mauboussin France." Courtesy of Fred Leighton.

From the mid-twentieth century onward, jewelers repeated these well-established designs and decorative motifs. Dior's New Look became successful after World War II and brooches were in full feminine view. Floral, Victorian-inspired, gem-intense pieces took center stage. Whether created with diamonds or rhinestones, these ornaments sparkled glamorously on the lapels of wasp-waisted suits and dresses. The 1960s pins and brooches exploded with color and texture. Jagged edges and organic patterns carved into metal paralleled the emotional intensity that defined this turbulent decade. Mary Quant–like daisies were reinterpreted into every type of pin material, from plastic to wood. The 1980s invited bold, sculptural, and sparkling pieces that could be worn atop the square shoulders of a suit.

In the new millennium, laser technology has brought about changes in metalsmithing and gem cutting. New materials and techniques are being used, taking jewelry design to another level of refinement; for example, Francis Mertens works his brooches in diamond pavé and titanium, the lightest of all metals. It is the same material used to create Airbus aircraft. An unconventional metal to use for jewelry, titanium can be colored and molded into shapes that more traditional metals cannot. Lifting one of Mertens's jeweled sculptures is like holding a sparrow in the palm of your hand. Its grace and weightlessness are astonishing yet its vibrancy is undeniable. Such jeweled masterpieces promise remarkable brooches to come.

Titanium and diamond brooch
with micropavé-set diamonds;
2006. Courtesy of Francis Mertens.

Flower brooch by Chopard.
A 28-carat conch pearl
surrounded by pink, white, and
brown diamonds accented by
pink spinels and green
tsavorites, all mounted in yellow,
white, and rose gold; 2002.
Courtesy of Chopard.

Chapter 2

CRAFT

*H*ow is a brooch made? Where does the idea for a pin design come from? Old-world workshops, studio artisans, and even artists renowned for their painted or sculpted works have found themselves drawn to jewelry making, and, in particular, pins. Producing an enduring brooch design is neither straightforward nor casual. This is a dedicated art form, where a designer transforms an idea into a three-dimensional ornament that is both beautiful and functional. Pins and brooches must fit the human form, so scale is a very important consideration. The size of a brooch plays an important part in its design. Is it to be large or small? If it is large, will it be comfortable to wear? How does the human form figure into the practical aspects of a pin?

A sculptural brooch and sleek dress can have a powerful impression. Silver brooch by Alexander Calder; circa 1955. Courtesy of Primavera Gallery New York.

Art deco brooch mounted in platinum and set with diamonds, jadeite, rubies, emeralds, yellow sapphires, and enamel; circa 1920. Courtesy of Frances Klein.

These are considerations that a designer must first address before the piece can go into production. Next, the execution of that design must be feasible for the goldsmith or gem setter to carry out. In the end, a fully realized brooch isn't merely an ornament but a comprehensive design scheme that is unified within its own boundaries.

The eighteenth century was known as the "Age of Diamonds." Brooches were ornately set with these precious gems or diamond substitutes called paste (or *stras*), which were made from highly refractive lead crystal. These artificial gems were named for Georges-Frédéric Stras, a jeweler who perfected the technique of creating simulated gems sometime around 1734. Paste stones are regularly

found in jewelry from this period and could be used to great effect since they shown as brilliantly under candlelight as the diamonds they imitated.

Eighteenth-century brooch design is an idiom of lush motifs of ribbon bows and floral forms. The jewelry of this period is also identified by a metalsmithing technique known as *cannetille* work in which wire is thinly scrolled and twisted into rosettes and complex filigree patterns that resemble lace embroidery. Unlike the previous century, the jewelry lexicon of the nineteenth century altered with each stylistic revival.

Beginning with romanticism, nineteenth-century adornment infused jewelry with motifs found in classical, Gothic, Etruscan, Asian, and rococo decorative arts. Renaissance-inspired brooches depicted enameled putti and heraldic themes, or weaponry motifs inspired by the Napoleonic War. Architectural elements were replicated in precious metal and framed jeweled portraits. After Queen Victoria became Empress of India in 1876, jewelry design was imbued with an exotic quality that was influenced by Indian and Far Eastern cultures.

Throughout the 1800s, naturalism reigned over the brooch form, with corsage ornaments boasting lifelike bouquets of gems set *en tremblant*; the blooms, which were mounted on gold wires, would tremble and shimmer in candlelight. This type of brooch was worn for only the most formal occasions. The effect must have been spectacular when women wore all their finery. Brooches often were one of the mainstays of a fashionable woman's wardrobe and were commonly part of a suite of jewels known as a *parure*.

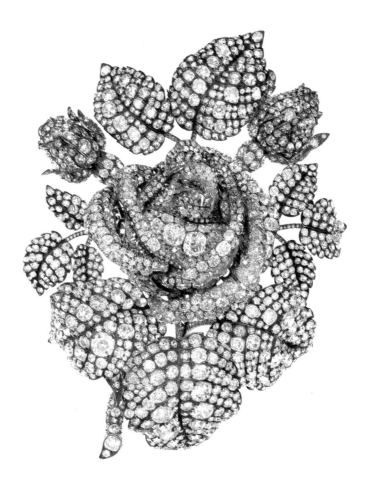

Diamond "Corsage" brooch by Theodore Fester. A large rose
blossom mounted in silver-topped gold and set entirely in diamonds;
circa 1855. This ornament was owned first by Princess Mathilde,
the daughter of Napoleon Bonaparte's brother Jerome. In 1904 it was
sold to Mrs. Cornelius Vanderbilt by Louis Cartier. Photograph by
Doug Rosa. Courtesy of Siegelson New York.

Toward the end of the nineteenth century, practically every visit to a museum exhibition or extended travel to Europe was commemorated with the purchase of a souvenir that attested to a person's worldly wanderings. Classical decorative motifs found in ancient Greek and Roman ruins were reproduced and crafted into ornaments that became known as archaeological jewelry. This style of adornment was pioneered by Fortunato Pio Castellani. His Etruscan-revival and reproduction jewelry resurrected an ancient and nearly lost gold technique called granulation, in which minute spheres of gold are flawlessly affixed to a metallic surface. The micromosaic brooch also became popular; these were tesseraed treasures depicting ancient ruins that were mounted in beautifully worked gold frames.

The brooch is an ideal medium to showcase the jeweler's art. It is a small but finite composition. Yet within that tiny framework, inspiration as bold as any life-size painting captivates its audience. The nineteenth-century jewelry firms of Castellani, Fabergé, and Lalique produced brooches that are still considered masterpieces today. The Castellani family, an Italian jewelry dynasty, created archaeological-style ornaments from the middle of the century until well into the twentieth. They manufactured and reproduced Etruscan jewels found in the Regolini-Galassi, Barberini, and Bernardini tombs. Castellani also cataloged and repaired all the gold work of the celebrated Campana collection, which contained some of the finest examples of ancient Greek, Roman, and Etruscan jewelry in the world. The techniques used to create these pieces,

Archaeological-revival gold and chalcedony cameo brooch by
Castellani; circa 1880. Photograph by Doug Rosa. Courtesy of
Siegelson New York.

OLD-WORLD CRAFTSMANSHIP
MEETS THE TWENTY-FIRST CENTURY
OSCAR HEYMAN & BROTHERS

FINE craftsmanship is the cornerstone of any jewel that transcends time and place. Skills were passed down from grandfather to father to son. Jewelry made in these well-established workshops was respected and highly desired so much so that extant pieces today remain collectible and valuable. Yet as the twentieth century progressed and technology in jewelry making improved, traditional handcrafting skills began to seem like a quaint but unnecessary process and interest in apprenticing waned. Formally trained metalsmiths can still be found in modern-day ateliers.

A jeweler's bench at the Oscar Heyman & Brothers workshop. An orchid brooch, based on an award-winning design from the 1939 World's Fair, is in the process of being set with gemstones. Photograph by David Behl. Courtesy of Oscar Heyman & Brothers, Inc.

However, it takes years to perfect their skills to the point at which they can be considered master craftspeople.

Happily there are jewelry houses that continue to work in the old-world traditions. Oscar Heyman & Brothers has been known as the "jeweler's jeweler" for nearly a century. Located in the heart of New York City, its workshop is perched above the hustle and bustle of Madison Avenue. On squeaky, wooden-planked floors, traditional and modern manufacturing equipment co-exist like mismatched dance partners. Jewelers and gem setters hunch over their benches focusing on the task before them with keen intensity. Modern technology has made it possible for pins to be manufactured by the dozens; however, that isn't necessarily where jewelry-making artistry is cultivated. When watching these bench jewelers in the twenty-first century, one can't help but feel that time has stood still. The brooches created in this workshop are made using the same metalsmithing techniques and gem-setting skills that jewelers have employed for centuries.

Custom-made pins are similar to couture dresses, as ideas are drawn from both the designer and the client for whom the piece is intended. There are many sources of inspiration and crafting an item of this quality is a multidimensional, labor intensive, and time-consuming process. Commonly, the suggestion for a design comes from a retailer like Oscar Heyman & Brothers or the client. Companies such as this one maintain vast libraries that are filled with reference books that their designers revisit periodically for additional ideas.

Rough drafts are then sent to the client who chooses the brooch to be made. Thereafter, a hand-painted rendering of the design is created. Every brooch produced is then fully realized in the form of a three-dimensional wax model, handmade by the company's designers. This is a wonderful way for the client to understand what the brooch will look like as a sculptural object and as a wearable jewel. A model takes anywhere from three days to a week to produce and is painted to replicate the metal and gems with which it will be set. If the design will include a large gem, this is also mounted into the wax model so that the client can see exactly how the stone will be featured in the setting.

Upon client approval the piece is produced. Every stage requires another set of expert hands. After the mounting is created and each gem is selected to fit the newly crafted setting, there is the labor-intensive polishing of every surface. The brooch then goes to the engraver and when he has completed his task, the piece returns to the polisher for one last shine. The company says a finished pin can take anywhere from six weeks to six months, depending on its complexity.

Daffodil brooch by Oscar Heyman & Brothers, Inc. Mounted in platinum and gold and set with fancy golden yellow and white diamonds; 2007. Courtesy of Oscar Heyman & Brothers, Inc.

Orchid brooch by Oscar Heyman & Brothers, Inc. Mounted in gold and set with fancy yellow and white diamonds; 2007. Courtesy of Oscar Heyman & Brothers, Inc.

"Le Baiser" (The Kiss) by René Lalique. Mounted in patinated silver and set with stained pressed glass. Lalique, Paris, circa 1904-06. Photograph courtesy of Lalique.

nearly lost over time, are the last remnants of the sophisticated aesthetic found in ancient adornment.

Russian crown jeweler Peter Carl Fabergé is credited with being one of the first designers to advance the idea of jewelry design as a commodity with monetary value. Traditionally, gems and precious metals were evaluated only in terms of their intrinsic value—a mere tally of their size and weight. The firm is renowned for its use of *guilloché* enamel, a technique whereby the gold or silver mounting is engine-turned on a lathe to create a pattern that can be seen through the transparent enamel. Fabergé used over 140 colors, many of which were only employed once and some of which, depending on the angle of light, could display more than one color. The formulas developed for these enamels were a closely guarded secret and very few were rarely duplicated.

Fabergé was also a pioneer in the use of platinum, a relatively new metal for jewelry manufacture. Pairing time-honored craftsmanship with new technologies, his workroom produced brooches where the interplay of platinum, gold, and gems resulted in something more than just the creation of an object of desire; this was art. Platinum swags and bows and floral designs now took on a delicacy that mimicked silk ribbon or a hand-painted bouquet. This achievement propelled the use of platinum well into the twentieth century.

Seeking artistic freedom, jewelers including René Lalique, Georges Fouquet, Henri Vever, and Lucien Gaillard used nontraditional materials to achieve mesmerizing effects in art nouveau jewelry. Incorporating enamel, glass, horn, ivory, mother-of-pearl, and semiprecious and precious stones, these artists created jewels admired for their painterly use of color and texture.

In Lalique's bejeweled world, women sprout brilliantly enameled *plique-à-jour* wings. Lovers are poised to kiss and the moment is forever captured on a slice of crystal and bound within the borders of intertwined branches of darkened silver. Lalique made brilliant use of *plique-à-jour* enamel, a technique that gave a stained-glass-like effect to the jewel. His penchant for incorporating unusual materials provided him with a broader palette of expression. A romantic landscape of a snow-laden forest, depicted on a pin-pendant, was achieved to superb effect through the use of enamel, glass, and gems. His influence was keenly felt by American jewelers Louis Comfort Tiffany and Marcus & Company, both of whom produced unique interpretations of art nouveau brooches.

By the turn of the twentieth century, the use of platinum was commonplace. Previously, this metal was viewed as difficult to work with due to its density; the advent of a high-temperature jeweler's torch changed this. Adornments, including pins and brooches, took on the look of white lace. With incandescent light, the diamond-cutting industry was forced to rethink its methods; old mine-cut stones, originally meant to be seen in candlelight, just did not scintillate the eye as well as the new-and-improved cut gems. From the Edwardian period to well into the 1930s, brooches and pins were about white metal and scads of large, brilliant gems. It was not until the 1940s that jewelry would return to its golden character.

Multicolored-gemstone flower brooch set with gold, pink, and blue sapphire, green and pink tourmaline, citrines, amethyst, moonstone, ruby, and blue zircon. American, circa 1940. Courtesy of James Robinson, Inc.

Art deco waterfall clip/brooch by Cartier. Mounted in platinum and set with diamonds; circa 1935. Collection of Randi and Jim Williams, courtesy of Williams Galleries, Nashville.

Flower brooch with articulated petals. Mounted in platinum and set with aquamarines, sapphires, and diamonds; circa 1950. Courtesy of Fred Leighton.

Cartier's panther motif has been reinvented over the decades. The motif makes for a pin that is endlessly chic. Model wearing Cartier diamond-briolette-and-sapphire "Panther" brooch. Photograph by Arthur Elgort/Vogue, © Condé Nast Publications Inc.

During World War II, all non-military use of platinum was banned. Gold was still available in limited quantities but was alloyed with copper, turning it a feminine shade of pink. Jewelers had to be clever with these precious materials and they hammered and pressed the metal into large, thin sheets so that the jewelry they created would have an expansive, important look. Pins sporting geometric lines appeared powerful and mechanized.

After 1945, romantic themes inspired by Victoriana reappeared: flowers, birds, animals, bows, ribbons, scrolls, and lace. Dior's wasp-waisted suits and dresses prompted the creation of exciting new brooches. The newly curvaceous shape of clothing was a wonderful foil to the bejeweled pin. Exuberance in jewelry design and in brooches in particular had returned; dimensional pieces with a presence took center stage. At this time Jean Schlumberger opened his atelier and designed the famous "Crown of Thorns" brooch for oil heiress and jewelry-collector-cum-designer, Millicent Rogers. Another 1940s masterpiece was Cartier's three-dimensional "Panther" brooch, a gift commissioned in 1948 by the Duke of Windsor for his wife. The inspiration for this iconic piece came from Cartier's jewelry-department head, Jeanne Touissant. Known for her ultra-chic style, Touissant had a penchant for all things exotically feline and her nickname around the atelier was "panther."

Brooches during the 1950s had a glamorous appeal where pear- and marquise-shaped stones were asymmetrically set and highlighted every facet. By the 1960s, these silhouettes exploded into designs that embodied the ongoing dialogue started by artist-jewelers decades before.

JEWELRY COLLECTOR-CUM-DESIGNER

MILLICENT ROGERS

SOMETIMES the client becomes the pin designer. This was the case with the stylish and creative Millicent Rogers, who had an exceptional understanding of the symbiotic relationship between adornment and fashion. She was rarely seen without her jewelry; among her favorites were brooches. As a client of world-renowned jewelers Cartier, Verdura, and Schlumberger, Rogers developed a connoisseur's eye for craftsmanship and artistry. She started creating her own jewelry, quietly emerging as a profound, self-assured designer for whom imperfect organic objects served as inspiration.

Millicent Rogers wearing a cape by Valentina. Her brooch is prominently placed and worn with eloquent style. Photograph courtesy of the Estate of Valentina Schlee.

"Arcturus" brooch designed by Millicent Rogers. Silver. This piece was part of a grouping of pins that Rogers entitled "Stars Running."

"Cloud Mountain" brooch by Millicent Rogers. Mounted in silver, copper, and brass.

No jeweler would dare mix precious and semi-precious stones in a single composition. However, Rogers was fearless and combined these stones with reckless abandon. She didn't care what other people thought about her jewelry—the only client she set out to please was herself. This attitude applied to how she wore her

pins, too. In 1947, when she moved to Taos, New Mexico, she began acquiring Native American artifacts, much of which was jewelry. She also started to design her own highly original pieces; brooches were among her favorites. "She was very arbitrary," notes her son, Arturo Peralta-Ramos. "She would take her pins and mix them with anything—whether it was a Navajo blouse or a Balenciaga gown."

During her travels, Rogers walked along the beaches or through the forests of the places she was living and collected objects. Nature's discards became the inspiration for brooches. "When she was living in the Austrian mountains, she found a pinecone with snow on it and said, 'Wouldn't that be pretty on a green or blue blouse,'" he recalls. Peralta-Ramos admires the great care his mother took in developing her designs. "She did her drawings in pencil, crayon, or pastels. Once drafted, she'd make the image smaller—the size of the jewel she wanted to wear—and then she drew it to scale." Her pins had a trademark practicality to them—they could be worn upside down or right side up. In fact, one remarkable clip she created was an ear of corn with the husk partially peeled back to display yellow and white diamond corn kernels. Mounted in gold with delicate corn silk crafted from spun silver, the entire brooch was set on a swivel so that she could adjust and orient the brooch in any direction.

Georgia O'Keeffe wearing her "OK" pin by Alexander Calder. Photograph by Cecil Beaton, 1967/Vogue, © Condé Nast Publications Inc.

Enamel brooch by Earl Pardon. Mounted in sterling with enamel on fine silver, and set with blue topaz, citrine, and amethyst; circa 1987. Courtesy of Aaron Faber Gallery.

Other perspectives are provided by established painters and sculptors, each of whom applied his or her skills to jewelry design. Surrealist painter Salvador Dalí and sculptor Alexander Calder expressed his or her art as jewelry. Envisioning brooches from their well-honed aesthetic was simply creating art from precious metal and gems instead of paint or clay. In about 1937 Dalí designed his first jewelry collection with fashion designer Elsa Schiaparelli; later he would work with the renowned designer Fulco di Verdura. From 1949 to 1960, Dalí designed for jewelry manufacturer Alemany to create his famous "Ruby Lips," which is now revered as a classic that continues to attract an audience because of its eccentric originality.

Calder readily admitted that his famous wire sculptures were inspired by the jewelry-making techniques he employed to shape pins, earrings, necklaces, and tiaras. In fact, his jewelry was regularly exhibited alongside his art. Most of these ornaments were created between 1933 and 1952.

Calder pounded out brass wire, although occasionally he would also employ gold or silver, bending it into rhythmic swirls that suggested figural, primitive, or symbolic motifs. He never used solder and instead would wrap or rivet additional elements to the main structure. In the beginning, the artist gave these trinkets to friends, but they became so popular that he eventually accepted commissions. Georgia O'Keeffe was notably photographed wearing her "OK" pin, a gift from the sculptor.

Mussel brooch by artist Daniel Brush. Mounted in gold and African blackwood and set with pearls, emeralds, and rubies; circa 1980. Courtesy of The DeYoung Collection.

This brooch, designed by artist Jean Lurçat and produced by Patek Philippe, was crafted with two colors of gold: yellow-green for the body and pink for the face; circa 1960. Courtesy of Primavera Gallery New York.

Although Calder started making jewelry in the 1930s, his hand-wrought pins foretold of the jewelry created by modernists from the 1940s through the 1950s. Similar to the artistic directive of the late-nineteenth-century Arts and Crafts movement, American studio jewelers rejected the idea of mass-produced, commercially made adornment. These craftspeople focused on the design ingenuity of their art rather than the intrinsic value of the materials with which it was fashioned. Several of these metalsmiths and jewelers received their training after serving in World War II. As a form of rehabilitation, recovering soldiers were taught basic jewelry-making techniques as a therapy to strengthen hand and arm muscles, and the G.I. Bill of Rights made it possible for veterans to go to college tuition-free; many studied metalsmithing.

Modernists from this period, such as Art Smith and Sam Kramer, favored biomorphic forms that had an organic quality. Smith's work was bold and massive; it possessed a highly sophisticated African tribal character with darkened patinas or stones caged within wire. Kramer had a surrealist bent in which an unsettling element was an integral feature of his brooches. The modernist perspective spoke of rhythmic shapes or asymmetrical voids and planes where the language of art in metalsmithing was interpreted between the lines rather than in a familiar representational form. An artisan who was trained as a painter, Earl Pardon, taught enameling at Skidmore College in Saratoga Springs, New York. His enameled brooches have an intoxicatingly colorful appearance that immediately draws the viewer in (see page 65).

REPRODUCTION AND ADAPTATION JEWELRY

JOANNE LYMAN, THE METROPOLITAN MUSEUM OF ART

*A*FTER thirty-three years of designing jewelry for The Metropolitan Museum of Art, Joanne Lyman understands the intricacies of producing a brooch. As a woman who wears jewelry, Lyman addresses some basic points: How will the pin be worn or what is the best season for the item? Is the ornament meant for a coat or dress? Large brooches need a thicker textile for support and work best on wool coats or chunky sweaters. She also considers if this is a cyclical accessory or one that can be worn year-round. "Just changing the scale of the piece can turn it into a spring item. Size also determines the appeal of a piece. I took a single earring to the photocopying machine and enlarged it and thought the design would make a great pin. The copier is a very useful tool."

Yet, she warns that color can be tricky. By varying the scale of the piece, hues can become harshly exaggerated, or they can do just the opposite and bring a pin to life. Adapting a pin design from a Tiffany ceiling ornament became a lesson in texture and color. After viewing the manufactured piece in photographs, Lyman discovered that the ornament needed some sparkle to break up the solidity of the surface. "We sprinkled it with Mylar and then fired it, which gave the pin iridescence. This adds color in an unfixed way that leaves the appeal in the eye of the beholder."

One of the pins Lyman is most proud of is the northern Renaissance pin-pendant she adapted from an original northern European jewel that dates from 1650, when diamond-cutting technology was still in its infancy. During the Renaissance, diamonds were cut more simply and had fewer facets, which greatly affected their brilliance. To the twenty-first-century eye they appear grayish when compared to the brilliant whiteness of a contemporary cut diamond. Trying to re-create the look of these early diamond cuts was challenging, Lyman remembers. "We couldn't use cubic zirconia because it was too vivid. So I found a darker-hued Austrian crystal that imitated the look of early diamonds." Since the variety of tones in manufactured crystal can be controlled to a greater extent, she was able to find a white-gray color that was comparable to that of the gems in the original seventeenth-century object.

In jewelry manufacture, the right details can have an enormous impact on a piece. In adaptation or reproduction jewelry, specific details, like the color or cut of a gem, must be simulated in a way that either imitates or strongly suggests the original. In order to capture the essence of an antique or vintage piece, the designer must consider the overall effect achieved as well as the separate elements that went into creating it. Thanks to her many years of experience, Lyman has learned this lesson and she is unquestionably a master of her craft.

Northern Renaissance pin/pendant by The Metropolitan Museum of Art. This ornament is based on a design in the museum's collection of jewels from northern Europe; circa 1620-1650. It is mounted in 24-karat-gold plate that has been lightly antiqued, decorated with hand-applied enamel, and set with Austrian crystals. Courtesy of The Metropolitan Museum of Art, New York.

Up until this point, the discussion of pin craft has solely been devoted to jewelers who designed brooches using virgin materials. Yet pins have also been made from old and recycled gems, mountings, or the frameworks of vintage pieces. Aided by an unerring eye for quality, Harry Winston started out in business by purchasing impressive examples of antique and estate jewelry. He would then remove the magnificent old stones, sometimes recutting and setting them into contemporary mountings. Costume- and set-designer Tony Duquette later transformed his larger-than-life aesthetic into boldly textured adornments with the occasional relic seamlessly woven into the mix. For today's designers, the idea of recycling remnants of estate jewelry is not only a practical concept but also one that gives old-world craftsmanship and materials renewed purpose and an audience to appreciate them in a contemporary way.

"Le Coeur" (The Heart) by artist Dorothea Tanning. This pin was mounted in gold and handcrafted by François Hugo. Collection of Deborah J. Gardner.

"Votive Heart" by Tony Duquette. This jewel was crafted using stones and elements from antique Chinese jewelry and 1930s retro jewelry, including a pink tourmaline heart-shaped cabuchon, lapis lazuli, azurite, caliber-cut turquoise, and diamonds. Set with 18-karat gold flame and sunburst motifs; circa 1960s. Courtesy of Tony Duquette, Inc.

Chapter 3

COLLECTING

*H*OLLYWOOD screen legend Elizabeth Taylor has gathered an impressive collection of brooches during her life. Many are mementos with personal meaning. "I have some 'important' pieces and others are just pretty. I value each one for its connection to someone I love and who loves me in return." When discussing her pins, she speaks of those she has a special fondness for, in particular the art nouveau and animal brooches that she has acquired.

Like Taylor, many collectors are passionate about brooches. The design is the primary attraction; there are as many motifs for brooches as there are fans of them. Typically there is a remarkable story about how each ornament reached the hands of its present owner. How it was discovered, acquired, or bestowed becomes as meaningful as the piece itself.

A clever arrangement of vintage pins can offer an effect as dramatic as a single important brooch.
Collection of Pam Sommers.

Eye miniature. Mounted in gold and set with almandine garnets and pearls surrounding a watercolor portrait of an eye. English, circa 1810. Courtesy of S. J. Shrubsole.

One such jewel is especially important to Taylor. "Richard [Burton] had just finished shooting *Night of the Iguana* in Mexico, and we took a trip to New York to let our tans fade," recalls Taylor. "We happened to go to Tiffany & Co. to cruise around and went to the top floor where they kept Mr. Schlumberger's staggering collection. They brought out a gold and diamond brooch and we looked at each other. I said, 'It's the iguana.' Well, it was just too much of a coincidence—one that Richard couldn't resist."

A venerable jewelry house or well-established retailer is a wonderful place to experience a great brooch; however it is important to remember that they are not the only sources for fabulous finds. You can discover great examples in flea markets, tag sales, and antiques malls. What you select has to satisfy no one other than yourself, and choosing wisely will always enhance your enjoyment of the piece. But be forewarned that the hunt can be addictive. Motifs run the gamut from insects to abstract sculpture. There are avid collectors of vintage brooches who seek out the artistic expression of a specific period like art nouveau, art deco, or 1940s retro. As the distance of time grows between the last quarter of the twentieth century and the beginning of the twenty-first century, the greater the appeal of brooch designs from the 1960s and 1970s. These decades are having a renaissance in popularity. A new generation of pin fans is discovering the bold, kinetic energy of these pieces. Fashion, too, helps to resurrect a taste for period pieces, building interest in items that speak not only of their own time but also integrate effortlessly into our own. Brooches collected over a lifetime are souvenirs that mark the milestones, celebrations, and travels of their owners. Their age becomes a fundamental part of their value and beauty. The much-handled areas of the metal form a patina that makes each object more desirable to the next person who acquires it, as the romance of the association gilds the ornament with an inimitable mystique. Fine examples of antique pins and brooches are always sought by collectors. Particularly rare are portrait miniatures that commemorated births, engagements, marriages, and deaths. These were pin-pendants that contained watercolor or oil renderings of the countenance of a family member or cherished friend. The custom of giving them as gifts was practiced regularly in England from the sixteenth century to the beginning of the twentieth. Most of the depictions were of kings and queens, as well as other affluent society.

Pins and brooches from the Georgian period (1714–1830) are as desirable as they are rare. Many were set in silver-topped-gold and mounted in diamonds, pastes (a gem substitute with a high lead content that was nearly as brilliant as a diamond), or colored gemstones. Pin motifs were of the romantic and sentimental nature, and harps, flowers, and ribbon bows were common. Personal keepsakes, such as portrait miniatures and lover's eyes, were popular. This last ornament, a tiny, gem-set brooch containing a depiction of an eye, was the focus of much intrigue. The identity of the subject was known only to the owner of the jewel. The commissioning of this kind of jeweled ornament began with England's young Prince George IV,

Elizabeth Taylor wearing the "Night of the Iguana" brooch by Schlumberger for Tiffany & Co. Photograph by William Lovelace, 1967. Courtesy of Getty Images/Hulton Archive.

Scottish chalcedony and Cairngorm brooch. Mounted in gold. United Kingdom, circa 1875. Courtesy of James Robinson, Inc.

Ruser pixie pin. Mounted in gold and set with diamonds, rubies, emeralds, and pearls by William Ruser; circa 1967. Courtesy of Fred Leighton.

who ordered two eye portraits, one of his and a second of his paramour, Mrs. Fitzherbert. Only the prince knew who was peering at him so intently within the frame of that portrait. Thereafter, lover's-eye miniatures became quite fashionable. Revered for their artistry and romantic association, they are highly sought after today.

What other types of pins are collectors drawn to? Some themes resonate more strongly than others in the vintage field. Admirers of Victorian jewelry are swept up by the variety of decorative techniques used in nineteenth-century pieces that imitated Greco-Roman discoveries, Egyptian artifacts, and Asian influences. The most sought after periods for jewelry design are the Edwardian and art deco; they are unequaled in the demand for the finest examples, which are rare and costly. Other collectors pursue expertly crafted, signed costume pieces that have the look and feel of fine jewelry.

Renowned pin collectors, like Joan Rivers and Elizabeth Taylor, enjoy gathering pieces that have connections to royalty or were made by world-renowned jewelers. Part of Rivers's collection of brooches with a regal heritage is a turquoise-set Prince of Wales plume that was a gift to Queen Victoria from Prince Albert on the occasion of the birth of their son, Albert Edward (later Edward VII). Also among her acquisitions is a small initial pin that Queen Mary gave to her bridesmaids when she married George V of England.

Victorians loved collecting and were inspired by nature, art, archaeology, and almost anything related to leisure pursuits; much of this aesthetic is reflected in the motifs of the brooches worn during the nineteenth century. As the leading trendsetter of her time, Queen Victoria made pins the quintessential jewel of the period. In 1848 she purchased the Scottish castle, Balmoral. Wanting to share the Queen's enthusiasm for Scotland, tourists and natives collected Scottish pebble jewelry. These pins were engraved with ancient Celtic designs on gold or silver and mounted with colorful, polished agate, quartz, and jasper, semiprecious gems indigenous to the Scottish Highlands. Set in the center of many these brooches is a smoky quartz known as a Cairngorm, which takes its name from the mountain region where the stones are found.

Queen Victoria was also an enthusiastic admirer of cameos. At holiday time she would bestow a likeness of herself or Prince Albert carved in shell or gem upon a special recipient. These cherished masterpieces were carved by renowned Italian father-and-son gem engravers Tommaso and Luigi Saulini. After Prince Albert died, the Queen went into a permanent state of bereavement and mourning jewelry became a part of one's daily attire. Somber-hued materials such as tortoiseshell, lava, jet, bog oak, and ivory were used for these brooches. Much of this material was carved into cameos. Traditionally, these jewels have been viewed as sentimental pieces and were collected by those who appreciate their sweet, somber past. Yet in recent years, these mementos have been valued by younger collectors for their dark, mysterious style that pairs so well with urban-chic fashion trends.

Cameo collectors are a dedicated group, fascinated by the story told in stone or shell.

A cameo depicts a narrative beyond its chiseled crevices, providing a direct connection to the artisan who created it. Running your fingers over the cameo's surface is equal parts tactile and informative; while you admire the wonderfully carved surface before you, the artisan's talent can be felt under your fingertips. Napoleon's invasion of Italy in 1796 created renewed interest cameos, an art form that originated in antiquity. Napoleon was moved by their eloquent beauty and had several of the ancient examples he brought back with him mounted and displayed in his own collection. Later, he established a school for gem engraving in Paris, where carving anything from a valuable emerald to a humble seashell was held to the highest standard.

As described, any brooch connected to royalty becomes iconic—and the same is true for Hollywood celebrities. The tales of ownership are interwoven with the ornament and become

inextricably bound to it. Rodeo Drive jeweler William Ruser set gold and freshwater Mississippi pearls together to create his quirkily charming pixie pins, popular items that found their way into numerous celebrity jewelry boxes; Loretta Young and Ava Gardner both owned them. These imaginative pins celebrated American pastimes, holidays, favorite pets, Mother Goose rhymes, and life's milestones. Because these pins were crafted from pearls that were asymmetrical, no two pixies are alike. On rare occasions, a custom-made pin was ordered. When Priscilla Beaulieu married rock-and-roll royal Elvis Presley in Las Vegas on May 1, 1967, she was given a gem-set Ruser pin with a crowned

and bejeweled pixie; to signify that the king had married his queen.

When a brooch's history is especially important, collectors are drawn to it for reasons beyond its beauty. It's the search for the uncommon that satisfies their acquisitive natures. They search for rare designer names or anomalies in design that mark a new trend or style. Early-twentieth-century jewelry design was dominated by men. But Jeanne Boivin and Suzanne Belperron, two Frenchwomen, paved the way for female jewelry designers later in the century. The adornments these women created are rare and highly regarded; there are collectors who scour the globe to find them.

When Jeanne's husband René died in 1917, she took over his jewelry business. From that point on Madame Boivin was the sole force driving the success of the company. Her taste for supple fluidity was in direct contrast to the architectural planes and geometric margins that defined the previous art deco period. This made her jewelry both wearable and sought after by the stylish, creative, and avant-garde. Colette, Jean Cocteau, and Millicent Rogers were among her many admirers. A 1945 *Vogue* photograph shows Rogers in a black swathe of ruched fabric with a Boivin starfish pinned near her right shoulder—close enough to highlight her face. Very few examples of Boivin starfish remain in

Flower brooch by Suzanne Belperron. Set with chalcedony, sapphires, diamonds, and platinum, the ornament bears the inscription "Noël, 1937." This brooch was owned by the Lanvin family and is nearly identical to the one owned by Wallis Simpson, the Duchess of Windsor. Courtesy of Newcal Galleries, Ltd.

Boivin starfish. This ruby and amethyst brooch was designed by
Juliette Moutard for the house of René Boivin. Paris, 1938. Crafted by
Charles Profilet. Photograph by Doug Rosa. Private collection.

contemporary, private collections but when they are displayed at auction or in museum exhibitions, it is not difficult to understand how their languid and beautifully articulated rays, luminous cabochons, and sparkling gems retain a luxurious, modern eloquence.

Suzanne Belperron began working as a salesgirl for Boivin in 1921. Two short years later, she became a designer for the company. Later she left to join jeweler Bernard Hertz as his business partner. With a definitive and steadfast approach, she would now design jewelry according to her own principles. First, the jewelry had to suit the wearer from a physical standpoint as well as style sensibility. Each piece needed to have a relevance to the person wearing it. She was famous for creating the circa 1935 chalcedony, sapphire, and diamond suite of jewels for Wallis Simpson, the Duchess of Windsor. The set consisted of a pair of cuff bracelets, a pair of earrings, and a necklace with a removable clasp that could also be worn as a brooch. The quintessential Belperron jewel has a voluptuousness paired with an adept use of accent stones, and it's this balance of shape and texture that makes her pieces so pleasing to look at and handle. Belperron rarely signed her work and finding an old example is a treat for any collector.

Unanticipated finds are often made while searching for pins and brooches. I once came upon

Austrian fruit pin, with glass raspberries and leaves, and purple rhinestone accent. Austrian, circa 1880. Courtesy of Joolbait Jewels. Raspberries are a rare motif of this type of costume pin.

a lovely handcrafted pin made by the Forest Craft Guild, a little-known arts and crafts group that was active at the end of the nineteenth century.

I had never collected a piece of jewelry from this period and because of this wonderful brass pin with its hand-hammered and acid-etched surface, I've come to appreciate an entirely new area of collecting. If a pin speaks to you, make the purchase; it may offer perspectives you hadn't previously considered. The journey you take to find a brooch can sometimes be as noteworthy as the item you've discovered.

While strolling through a summer flea market, my cousin's curiosity was piqued by a table piled high with fruit pins, most of them made in Austria. Her connection to the vibrant objects was immediate, and now she's a keen collector of them. Luminous plums, strawberries, pears, and bunches of grapes are crafted from molded or carved glass awash in iridescent tones of blue, green, amber, red, and violet. Austrian fruit pins were made solely for sale to the United States in the 1940s and 1950s. Their simplicity speaks of a time when ordinary table fare was crafted into the most delicious of jeweled ornaments. Wearing a few demure cherries with a summer dress or pinning an entire fruit salad to your lapel is about expressing your own sense of style.

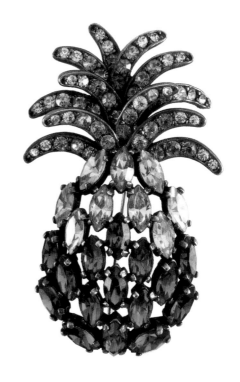

Costume pineapple pin with multicolored rhinestones by Schiaparelli; circa 1940. Courtesy of The RSL Collection.

COLLECTIONS

 HE selection of brooches presented here is merely a cross section of the thousands of motifs and styles gathered by collectors. Some are popular, others more esoteric, but all are wonderful. Many times the hunt can be more satisfying than the find. When presented together, a collection of pins and brooches reveals a compelling story of the style of the person who discovered it.

Diamond pin/pendant. Mounted in silver-topped-gold and set with natural-colored and white diamonds; circa 1880. Courtesy of The DeYoung Collection.

Nineteenth- and Early Twentieth-Century Ornaments

The Georgian period began in 1714 and continued into the early part of the nineteenth century. Late Georgian brooches are highly sought after by collectors for their elegant personality. Surviving over centuries, without having been substantially altered or destroyed, these rare ornaments remain fine examples of a bygone era. Typically, jewelry from this period features diamonds or white paste stones mounted in organic or romantic motifs. When Princess Victoria became Queen of England in 1837, jeweled ornaments followed the tastes and dictates of royalty. Styles ranged from multicolored Scottish pebble pieces inspired by the queen's home in Balmoral to the black- or dark-hued ornaments worn in mourning. After years of advances in the mechanization of jewelry manufacture, the end of the Victorian period brought about nostalgia for the hand-wrought object. Art nouveau and arts and crafts jewelry reflected a renewed appreciation for the art of the metalsmith and gem setter. Quality craftsmanship again was revered, as it had been a century earlier.

These three nineteenth-century *echelle* bodice ornaments are mounted in silver-topped-gold and set with sapphires and diamonds. The term *echelle* is used to refer to the series of graduating bodice or dress ornaments commonly worn in the seventeenth and eighteenth centuries. Courtesy of Fred Leighton.

Late Georgian/early Victorian collection. Clockwise (from top left): Naturalistic wild-rose spray diamond brooch mounted in silver-topped-gold; circa 1860. Irish harp mounted in silver-topped-gold and set with old-cut paste; circa 1830. Lyre brooch mounted in silver-topped gold and set with pastes; circa 1820. Diamond bow and drop mounted in silver-topped-gold; circa 1840. Stylized daisy brooch with petals of old-cut diamond mounted in silver and gold; circa 1840. All courtesy of Olivia Collings Antiques.

Top: Cornucopia brooch.
Mounted in silver and gold, and
set with white and natural-
colored diamonds, pearls, rubies,
and an emerald. The body of this
exquisite cornucopia is a large
rose-cut diamond. This piece
was part of an impressive
collection of jewels owned by
opera singer Ganna Walska;
mid-nineteenth century.
Courtesy of The DeYoung
Collection. Bottom: Sampler pin
by Boucheron. Mounted in
platinum, and set with seed
pearls, rubies, emeralds,
sapphires, and diamonds.
French, circa 1920. Courtesy
of Fred Leighton.

Victorian Scottish pebble
jewelry. Top: Butterfly. Mounted
in sterling silver and set with
well-matched examples of lace
agate; circa 1860. Bottom: Dirks
(long daggers). These three
ornaments are mounted in gold
and set with faceted citrines and
Scottish agates; circa 1860.
Courtesy of Linda Morgan
Antiques.

Arts and Crafts

Jewelry of this genre had several perspectives, one of which was the ever-evolving view of Georg Jensen and the company's many talented designers. Another was that of Edward Oakes, whose organic aesthetic typified the Boston school of arts and crafts style. Top: Floral brooch by Edward Oakes. Mounted in sterling silver and set with zircons. Boston, Massachusetts, circa 1920s or 1930s. Bottom: Brooch designed by Georg Jensen (design no. 122). Mounted in sterling silver. Demark, circa 1933. All brooches courtesy of Drucker Antiques.

Art Nouveau

Swans. Mounted in gold, decorated with *plique-à-jour* and basse taille enamels, and set with diamonds and rubies. Paris, circa 1900. Courtesy of James Robinson, Inc.

Heart-shaped brooch. Pierced gold, platinum, and diamonds. French, circa 1905. Courtesy of S. J. Shrubsole.

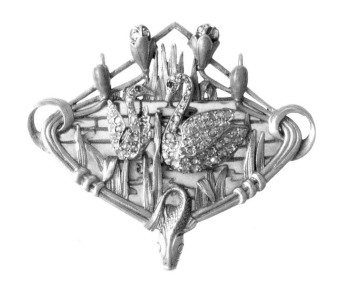

Costume Jewelry

Whether they adorn fine linen or calico, costume brooches are an easy way to add instant glamour or vivid color to an ensemble. Because they are not crafted from precious materials, designs are imaginative—with motifs ranging from geometrics to birds, bugs, and bouquets.

Pink flower costume pin by Boucher; circa 1945. Courtesy of the RSL Collection.

Costume pearl and rhinestone pins can look as impressive as fine jewelry. Floral rhinestone bouquet brooch; circular pearl pin with flowers; pearl pin with drops; and faux coral and turquoise pin. All courtesy of The RSL Collection. Swirl rhinestone clips. Collection of Cathie Klitin.

Azalea brooch: silver and copper over bronze with fresh water pearls; leaf: hand-patinaed bronze; 2007. Dogwood brooch: silver and copper over bronze; leaf: Hand-patinaed bronze; 2007. All courtesy of Silver Seasons.

Costume enamel pins and backdrop of grass green paisley. Courtesy of The RSL Collection.

Cameos

The sculpted planes of cameos recount classical
motifs. Their soft, luminous colors are derived from
shell or gemstone, where contrasting tones are
revealed between the surfaces and the exposed
layers beneath. As adornment, cameos have a poetic
serenity that often belies their impact.

Cupid cameo mounted in
silver-topped-gold and featuring
a diamond open shell. French,
circa 1820. Courtesy of Fred
Leighton.

White-gold mounted hardstone
cameo set with diamonds, by
James de Givenchy for Taffin;
2002. Courtesy James de
Givenchy for Taffin.

Top (left): Mounted in art nouveau gold frame with coral cameo; (right): gold-mounted hardstone cameo, set with diamonds and sapphires; Center: an Asian motif is carved into a lapis vase holding a bouquet of twelve shell and coral cameos interspersed with leaf motifs. Most of the cameos are Victorian and set in their original gold ring tops and stickpins. This piece was crafted during the 1940s, when Victoriana was enjoying a resurgence in popularity. Diamonds adorn a few of the cameo frames. Bottom (left): silver-topped gold mounted shell cameo set with diamonds. French, mid-nineteenth century; (center): Rose-gold-mounted sardonyx cameo carved with a figural mythological scene; mid-nineteenth century; (right): gold-mounted hardstone cameo decorated with black enamel tracery, and set with seed pearls. All courtesy of Lang Antiques.

These agate cameos in an Etruscan-revival gold mount depict, from left to right, the profile of a lady, a flying moth, and the profile of a man. Courtesy of Fred Leighton.

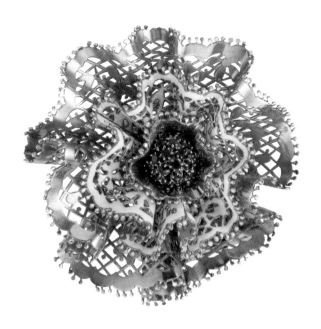

Feminine Motifs

Brooches with a feminine slant illustrate the beguiling side of ribbons, bows, and dancing ballerinas when they alight on the shoulder of a jacket.

"Dentelle" brooches by Van Cleef & Arpels. Mounted in gold and set with rubies; circa 1940. Courtesy of Fred Leighton.

Costume bow pin by Chanel; circa 1930–40. Courtesy of The RSL Collection.

Costume fan pin by Trifari. Courtesy of The RSL Collection.

Ballerinas. Top (left to right): Spanish dancer ballerina. Mounted in gold and set with rubies, sapphires, and diamonds; John Rubel. Tiptoe ballerina with wings. Mounted in gold and set with rubies, diamonds, and turquoise; unsigned. Ballerina with overhead ribbon. Mounted in gold and set with rubies, diamonds, and turquoise; Van Cleef & Arpels. Bottom (left to right): Sprite ballerina. Mounted in gold and set with rubies, diamonds, and sapphires; Van Cleef & Arpels. Cancan dancer. Mounted in gold and set with rubies, diamonds, and sapphires; John Rubel. Dancer with fan. Mounted in gold, and set with rubies, diamonds, and turquoise; unsigned. All private collection.

Clockwise (from the left):
Hat brooch. Mounted in gold
and set with multicolored pearls
and rose-cut diamonds; circa
1890. Enamel Japanese fan.
Mounted in gold and set with
rose-cut diamonds and oriental
pearl. French, circa 1885.
Basket-weave hat brooch.
Mounted in gold and set with
diamonds. French. Fan brooch.
Mounted in gold and set with
rubies, mine- and rose-cut
diamonds. All courtesy of Fred
Leighton.

Costume bow pin by Mazer. Red
and green enamel with white
paste bow accent. Courtesy of
Kentshire Galleries, Ltd.

Florals

Pinning a gardenia to your collar in mid-winter is a wonderful way to remind yourself that spring is just around the corner. Florals are blooms in perpetuity and will provide the flower fix you are seeking anytime of year.

Floral plaque pin. Mounted in platinum and set with rose diamonds, cabochon rubies, and sapphires. French, circa 1920. Courtesy of Frances Klein.

Platinum and diamond flower pin; circa 1950. Courtesy of Frances Klein.

Gardenia brooches by Oscar Heyman. Top: Mounted in gold and platinum, and set with white and yellow diamonds. Center (left): Mounted in gold and platinum, and set with white and yellow diamonds and green enamel leaves; (right): mounted in platinum and set with diamonds with green enamel leaves. Bottom: Mounted in platinum and set with diamonds and green enamel leaves. The top and center left designs were originally created in the 1930s; the entirely white flowers are contemporary pieces. All courtesy of Oscar Heyman & Brothers, Inc.

Left: A reverse intaglio crystal of an Airedale terrier. The crystal was carved and painted in England and the brooch was mounted in gold by an American jeweler; circa 1955. Courtesy of Hamshere Gallery.

Top: A reverse intaglio crystal of a head study of a Jack Russell terrier. Gold mounted. English, circa 1890. Bottom: A reverse intaglio crystal of a rare and historic head study of an English white terrier. Gold mounted. English, circa 1890. The English white terrier was a popular breed in the early 1860s. Within thirty years of appearing on the Kennel Club scene, the breed slipped into extinction. All courtesy of Hamshere Gallery.

Animals and Insects

Those with a penchant for dogs or hedgehogs can wear one on their lapel. Cats, birds, dogs, and butterflies are popular with collectors because of their clever representations. These pieces capture their audience when the beauty of beast is echoed brilliantly within the jewel.

Bird of paradise. Mounted in gold with enamel, and set with diamonds; circa 1965. Courtesy of Camilla Dietz Bergeron, Ltd.

Antique Italian micromosaic brooch by James de Givenchy for Taffin; 2002. Emerald-cut diamonds and spines. Courtesy of James de Givenchy for Taffin.

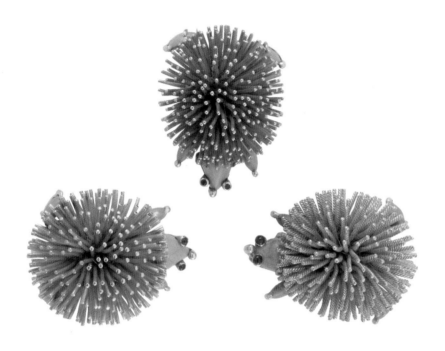

Hedgehogs. Mounted in gold
and set with turquoise and
rubies. Van Cleef & Arpels.
Private collection.

Turtle. Mounted in gold and
set with malachite, coral, and
turquoise; circa 1960. Courtesy
of Camilla Dietz Bergeron, Ltd.

Gold-mounted reverse intaglio
crystal of a head study of a tabby
cat set with natural pearls.
English, circa 1880. Cat motifs
are less commonly found in this
type of jewel than dogs.
Courtesy of Hamshere Gallery.

Kittens. Hand-chased gold set
with ruby and diamonds.
Courtesy of Fred Leighton.

Fox. Mounted in gold, enamel, and set with emeralds; David Webb; circa 1970. Courtesy of Camilia Dietz Bergeron, Ltd.

White-meerschaum- and black-rhodium-plated white-gold deer head set with diamonds and baroque spinel by James de Givenchy for Taffin; 2005. Courtesy of James de Givenchy for Taffin.

Costume tiger pin. Courtesy of
The RSL Collection.

Birds of a feather. Left: Bird in
plaque hanging from a bow and
terminating in three drops. Right:
Costume bird pin by Trifari.
Courtesy of The RSL Collection.

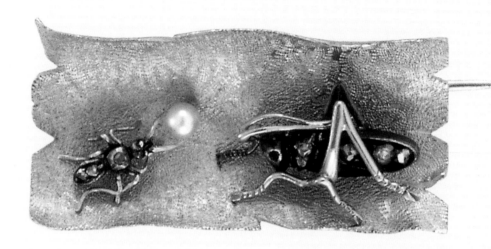

Perched on a gold log, the
grasshopper and fly are mounted
in gold and silver and set with
rose-cut diamonds, emeralds,
and a pearl. French. Courtesy of
Fred Leighton.

Collection of English Victorian
bugs mounted in gold using a
variety of materials, including
foil-backed crystal and agates.
The rose-cut diamond fly pins
are also set with moonstone,
emeralds, and ruby. Courtesy
of Linda Morgan Antiques.

Chapter 4

STYLE

A brooch conveys a message that is public, private, or unwitting. Whether this is an intended declaration or not, the minute it is pinned on the wearer exposes a bit of themselves. Holiday pins represent celebration and are simple to interpret. However, what if the brooch is an abstract design of lines and planes that examines spatial relationships? Or one that serves as a public notice, projecting a witty or political statement? Wearing a brooch should be a kind of self-expression, a way of revealing your individual style. The more you enjoy the ornament, the greater your pleasure will be in pinning it on and displaying it to the world.

Platinum and diamonds transform everyday wool flannel into something extraordinary.
Mounted in platinum and set with diamonds. Sterle, Paris, circa 1950. Courtesy of Fred Leighton.

Distinct from a necklace, bracelet, or ring, a brooch does not require the armature of the body for support. A pin can be attached to an item of clothing in order to incorporate it into an overall "look." There are those who spend as much time thinking about which brooch to choose and how to wear it as they do the outfit they plan to pair with it.

Occasionally a brooch is a decorative element of a necklace or bracelet. These adaptable jewels offer the wearer more than one way to enjoy them since the pin can be removed easily and worn separately. The sweater pin is as practical as it is pretty. Customarily used as a closure for a sweater, it transforms an ordinary button down into an

Sweater pin. Mounted in gold with green enamel, and set with old-mine- and rose-cut diamonds. English, circa 1890. Courtesy of Fred Leighton. A sweater pin, one of those old-school ideas, dresses up cashmere and lush fabrics so beautifully.

Gold bracelet with detachable diamond brooch. Courtesy of Fred Leighton.

elegant topper. Worn as an ornament, it has a personality of its own.

Avid pin collector Elaine Mack considers how to style an outfit with a brooch almost every day. As a personal shopper for Bergdorf Goodman, it is part of her job to know how to coordinate brooches with clothing. She uses them strategically; for example, when Mack slides a brooch over the knot of a fabric belt, she is placing focus at the waist. Worn up on the shoulder or high on a lapel, a clip draws attention toward the face in a refined and flattering way. "I have clients in their seventies and eighties who have fabulous antique pins that they always wear near their faces; it works to soften their overall appearance. This is especially true of period brooches, the ones that have a history."

Joan Rivers wears her pins with simple, beautifully cut suits or dresses with jackets. Her collection is an eclectic array of pieces that reflects her love of great design. "I collect all over the place, from Paul Flato to JAR," she explains. Despite the

Audrey Hepburn, 1957. Courtesy of the Everett Collection, Inc.
Pinning a brooch to a scarf or high upon the shoulder focuses subtle
but deliberate attention to the face.

A white jacket is sheer drama with this Harry Winston platinum
and diamond "Cluster" brooch on the lapel. Courtesy of Harry Winston.

Whether they are contemporary or estate piece, scatter pins have a charming appeal. When brooches of varying sizes are grouped together, they suggest a far more important appearance. Model wearing a Prada jacket accessorized with Harry Winston's garnet and diamond "Jackie O" brooch, Jean Schlumberger for Tiffany & Co. "Sea-flower" cultured pearl and diamond clip, and Van Cleef & Arpels' "Hawaii" clips set with amethyst, sapphire, rubellite, and diamonds. Photograph by Arthur Elgort/Vogue, © Condé Nast Publications Inc.

Pansy pins. Mounted in silver-topped-gold and set with diamonds; circa 1880. Courtesy of Frances Klein.

wonderful choices in her collection, Ms. Rivers says she doesn't wear her best pieces often. "These are treasures to be admired; but I can't put a Fabergé on a jean jacket." Instead, costume pins fill that niche very nicely; Rivers enjoys a random mix of glitzy options. Her pin philosophy ignores proportions of both the wearer and the ornament; drama is what counts. For anyone who has ever been put off by the scale of a brooch, this approach invites consideration. Give it a try; you might like the way it looks. A large brooch can add a touch of glamour to an everyday outfit; it can take you from the office to cocktails and dinner. But even Rivers draws the line. When asked what not to do with a pin or brooch, she offers up a cautionary tale, "Pauline Trigere was a wonderful designer but she would wear pins at her knees."

Wearing pins in unusual places may appear to be a bit over the top. However, you can still experiment with them. My grandmothers liked "scatter pins." These are clusters of pins grouped together on the shoulder of a jacket or sweater. Elaine Mack sees young girls like her granddaughter scattering them on jean jackets. Pins are accommodating little objects of inspiration. You can create a stronger impression by assembling them together rather than wearing them singly.

The only rule for a winning display of scatter pins is to have the pieces relate to one another. Rivers collects Victorian flower pins that she enjoys wearing together; she blends the real thing with the costume pieces from the collection she designs. In order to group them successfully, you should have an arrangement in mind. "It's like hanging paintings," says fashion stylist Ann Caruso. "If you are going to put together paintings or frames of varying sizes on a wall, you have to figure out how they will work together."

SCALE

Consider scale when grouping two or more pins together. Aim at creating a relationship with varying sizes. Large pins offer drama and an eye-catching presence when worn alone.

Left: "English Garden Pagoda" brooch. White topaz and gold with blue sapphire accents; 2007. Right: "Chinoiserie Pagoda" brooch. Kunzite and gold with diamond briolettes, pink sapphire, tsavorite garnet, and a pink cultured freshwater pearl; 2007. Courtesy of Mish New York.

Large jeweled courtier by Tony Duquette, using elements from a 1910 Cartier brooch. In the 1960s Duquette reset the original piece by adding gold, diamonds, pearl epauletes, and a crowned mask. Courtesy of Tony Duquette, Inc.

"Wing" pin by Garrard. Mounted in white gold and set with diamonds. Courtesy of Garrard.

While the shoulder and the lapel of a jacket are the most common locations for brooches, these pieces of jewelry offer great flexibility when it comes to situating them. The shoulder, the waist, or the low backline of a dress are all fair game. One of Garrard's recent creations is a brooch in the form of an angel's wing. This white gold and diamond brooch can be worn as easily in the hair, like a barrette, as it can as a closure for a bolero or sweater. In a pinch, a pin can function in place of a button or even a broken zipper. At an important fashion event, one stylist's jacket came apart when her zipper failed. She was wearing next to nothing underneath and needed a way to keep the jacket closed. Luckily, she had a wonderful costume pin in her purse. It was just something grabbed while leaving her hotel room for the evening.

Brooches can be worked into a look without much fuss, which is a key consideration when going from the office to an evening event. Just slip one into a handbag or tote so you can transform your look at a moment's notice. They can also be used in place of a belt buckle, like the sash brooches worn by women in the late 1800s into the early twentieth century. "When I'm on a shoot, I am limited as to what I can bring and brooches can be thrown on anything," says celebrity stylist Jeanne Yang. "They go as well on a ball gown as they do with a T-shirt and jeans." She often uses them to highlight the straps of a slip dress, quickly turning daywear into sparkling eveningwear. Using brooches in these interesting ways is not about extravagance; you can achieve any of these looks with either an expensive example or one found at a flea market. The goal is to use them in a practical or clever way; this way of styling is what sets brooches apart from all the other types of jewelry.

While recent fashion trends have flirted with the brooch as that "must-have" accessory, in truth it is much too useful an item to retire to the jewelry

A pair of "fruit salad" clips. Mounted in platinum and set with yellow and white diamonds, emeralds, rubies, sapphires, and star sapphires; circa 1930. Courtesy of Frances Klein.

This 1940s photograph shows Carole Lombard wearing a fabulous pair of gem-intense clips. The brooches add a glamorous and sparkling note to the slender straps of her gown. Courtesy of the Everett Collection, Inc.

CHOKERS AND NECKLACES

Traditionally, a pin was made with a bail (or loop) at the top or back so that it could also be worn as a pendant. Some contemporary brooches have a bail; a skilled repairperson can add one if desired. A costume brooch can make a great neckpiece too when pinned to a length of ribbon.

Marilyn Monroe needs nothing more than a precisely placed pin to show off her assets. Courtesy of the Everett Collection, Inc.

Art deco diamond and rock-crystal pendant necklace/brooch combination by Mauboussin, Paris, 1931. Courtesy of Siegelson New York.

These costume pins feature black enamel, milk glass, and white enamel with black polka dots. Their striking color palette and charming silhouettes convey a sense of playfulness that makes them the perfect foil for an unadorned length of ribbon. Collection of Gertrude Gramaglia.

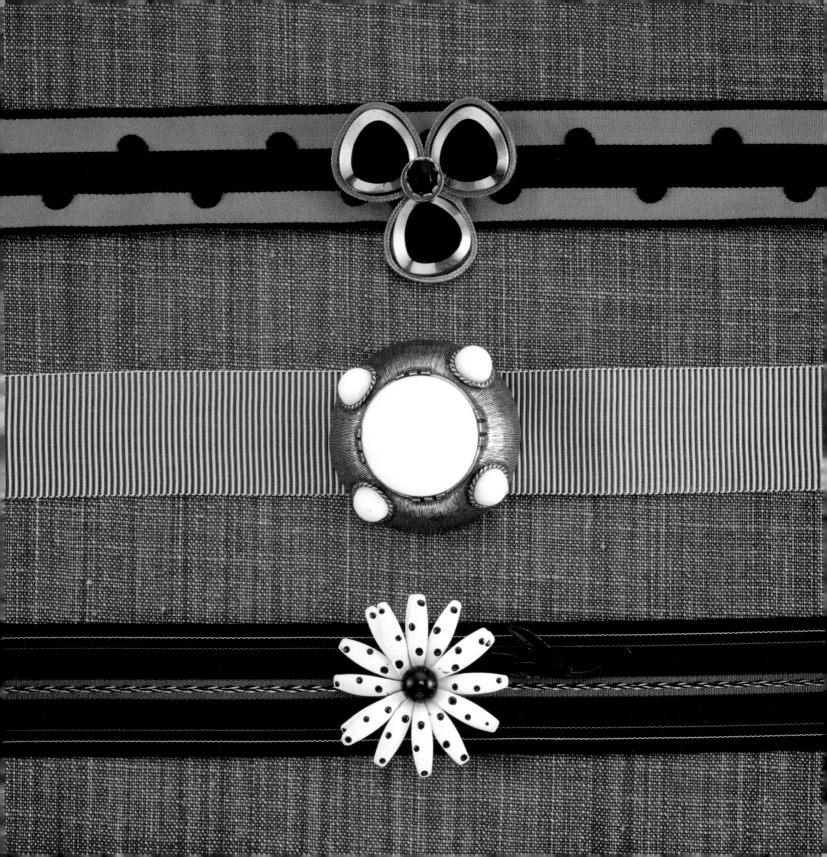

Hardstone cameo of a cherub riding a lion depicting "Love conquers all." English-crafted gold-mounted Italian cameo; circa 1820. Courtesy of Olivia Collings Antiques.

box or dresser drawer when it momentarily falls out of favor. Many older and some contemporary brooches have hidden bails (commonly known as a loop) that can be strung on a chain and be worn as pendants. A plain clutch can be transformed into a lovely evening accessory by simply pinning a great clip to the closure. Hats and shoes can be similarly adorned. Take a pin and attach it to a rubber band, then tie the band around a chignon for impromptu

elegance. The hem of a long skirt gets a lift when pinned up to reveal the leg, and balance is achieved by pairing a bulky knit with a long sculptural pin.

Brooches are a wonderful way to add color to an ensemble. Metallic shades and decorative techniques such as enamel offer many options; each has its own distinctive character. Then there are fabulous gems or paste brilliants to consider. "I have this red jacket and a great vintage costume brooch my mother-in-law left me," says Elaine Mack. "It's a huge gold flower with red stones in the middle of it and when I wear it, the color of both pieces jumps out at you."

A colorful pin can significantly alter the look of black, navy, or gray. When dressing her more conservative clients for suits, Mack suggests colored brooches to soften the austere appearance of a palette of neutrals. The traditional pinstriped suit takes on a whole new character when paired with something eye-catching on the lapel. Mack is also a cameo devotee. She notes, "If you have a brown plaid suit and a great cameo that has the same taupe/brown coloring to it, it makes the plaid pop and the brooch stand out."

Using a shell or stone cameo brooch for its fabulous color is refreshing. While they are commonly admired for their skillful carving, a cameo's neutral hue can add just the right amount of subtle color. Cameos also elicit a quiet luxury; they cast a kind of intellectual refinement upon the wearer. They are the type of jewels that do not roar but instead have a quiet dynamic much like an oil painting or classical sculpture.

Even if two people are wearing the same

pin, the way they wear it will offer clues about their personal style and perception of that ornament. My favorite pin was originally owned by my paternal grandmother. Born at the end of the nineteenth century, her taste leaned toward the Victorian, when jewelry was piled on in a more-is-more manner. Years later Coco Chanel took this Victorian-inspired look, refined the elements, and made it forever chic. My grandmother wore this pin together with a necklace or two, a watch, large earrings, and a pair of bangle bracelets. Nothing was actually coordinated, and I honestly can't ever recall picking out the pin among all the pieces in her dazzling array.

I like to wear her pin by itself. It is a wonderful example of nineteenth-century charm and grace. Ribbons of gold frame a medallion of cobalt blue enamel; a small, beautifully worked silver basket of rose-cut diamond flowers is mounted in the center of the brooch. When I wear it, the gems glitter softly, evoking their vintage splendor. My grandmother loved it as I do; only the way we choose to wear it differs. For her, it was part of a striking ensemble of gems and metals; for me, our brooch is a precious and lyrical antique that deserves undivided attention.

As in the case of my grandmother's pin, which was given to me by my mother, often brooches are handed down in families and serve as reminders of someone or something cherished. Many of these gifts are worn with great pride. It's always lovely to be asked about them and then to have the opportunity to recall the story of the journey this heirloom took before it was in the hands of the

Pin/pendant mounted in gold with cobalt blue enamel, and set with natural half pearls. Central floral silver basket motif set with rose-cut diamonds. French, nineteenth century. Author's collection.

next caretaker. Some pins possess wonderfully long and evocative stories; sadly, others just sit in a drawer for much too long before arriving on the shoulder of someone who loves them. Whether you received a brooch as an heirloom or a castoff makes little difference as long as you make it your own.

Chapter 5

PIN-OLOGY

*W*HEN perusing a fashion magazine, have you ever noticed a pin displayed to stunning perfection? Trying to emulate this effect is not difficult; the key is to keep it simple. Note how the brooch is used. Look at the fabric upon which the ornament sits and its position. Get an overall sense of composition; this should give you enough information to understand how the stylist achieved the look. Now translate that to your own fashion sense, and be creative. Inspiration taken from a magazine or book should be a point of departure rather than a destination.

Cushion-cut spessatite garnet, tourmaline, and diamond brooch by James de Givenchy for Taffin; 2004.
Courtesy of James de Givenchy for Taffin.

This chapter is intended to both indulge the eye and offer ideas. The English suffix "ology" means "the study of," so consider this section a primer on pin pairing. Notice how tweed works with Victoriana, or white metal and diamonds appear majestic on a fur-trimmed collar. Study the effect produced when an ornament and fabrication work in tandem. Enameled portraits become richer on a backdrop of beige wool flecked with white, black, and brown.

The illustrations have been divided into themes: color, faces, flora, whimsy, aquatic, curvilinear, and unconventional materials. A whimsical pin constructed from origami paper can have as much impact as one made from gold. Costume pieces often are as beautiful as those mounted in precious materials; a glamorous effect can be achieved with either. Flowers can be stylized or naturalistic; color plays an important role in their perception. Circles throw a curve on the subject. Ocean themes recall relaxing pastimes and sunny places so they work as well on a tablecloth plaid as they do on a silk weave.

There are no hard and fast rules with this form of adornment; the images presented here are merely suggestions. It's about wearing this kind of jewelry traditionally or not; experimentation is always encouraged. When you add your own thoughts to the mix, the results will be picture perfect.

Have fun with pins. Pluck one down on hat, coat, or handbag; its whimsy will immediately elevate the mood. Model wearing wool coat and tweed hat with Giorgio Armani brooch. Photograph by Patrick Demarchelier/Vogue, © Condé Nast Publications Inc.

Platinum and diamond circles pin; circa 1920. Courtesy of Frances Klein.

Bow brooches. Mounted in platinum and set with onyx and diamonds; circa 1920. Courtesy of Frances Klein.

Floral brooch by Van Cleef & Arpels. Mounted in yellow gold and set with diamonds and emeralds; circa 1950. Courtesy of Frances Klein.

Platinum and diamond feather brooch; circa 1945. Courtesy of Frances Klein.

COLOR

*T*HE spectrum of light that the eye perceives and the mind ponders defines color. Flowers, rainbows, and other silhouettes cue us to context. Black and white, a monochromatic alignment, underscores shape and structure. Opposition gives way to perspective.

Multicolored gemstone brooch by Chanel. Designed by Coco Chanel and made in the Verdura workshop, this prime example of 1930s glamour is set in gold, aquamarine, sapphires, citrines, amethysts, and peridot or emeralds, possibly both; circa 1935. Courtesy of Primavera Gallery New York.

Retro flowers. Mounted in gold, and set with multicolored sapphires, pink tourmalines, and diamonds. Cartier, circa 1945. Courtesy of Newcal Galleries, Ltd.

A pair of "Lotus Flower"
brooches by James de Givenchy
for Taffin. Mounted in platinum
and set with rubelite and
amethyst; 2001. Courtesy of
James de Givenchy for Taffin.

Flower brooch, Lucite; 2007.
Courtesy of Alexis Bittar.

BLACK AND WHITE

No palette is more dramatic than black, white, and gray. Left to right: "Tidal" brooch by Sydney Lynch.
Oxidized sterling silver and gray pearls; 2007. "Grid and Decoration" brooch by Marianne Anderson.
Oxidized sterling silver and button pearls; 2007. "Nightness" brooch by Tod Pardon. Sterling silver, gold, ebony,
simulated ivory, turquoise, and mixed inlay; 2003. All courtesy of Aaron Faber Gallery.

Circular pin. Mounted in platinum and set with diamonds and calibre-cut onyx.
English, circa 1925. Courtesy of The DeYoung Collection.

FACES

A smile or a stare describes a mood. This kind of ornament is an artistic expression of the human condition. The pin tells a story or prompts one.

Enamel portraits. Clockwise (from top left): Woman's profile with Egyptian headdress. Gold and enamel. Young girl with blue hat and muff. Gold, enamel, and rose-cut diamonds. Woman's profile with Renaissance dress. Gold, enamel, and rose-cut diamonds. Woman's profile in jeweled and scalloped frame. Gold, enamel, old-mine diamonds, and pearls. Bearded man with red cap. Gold, enamel, old-mine and rose-cut diamonds, and seed pearls. Center: Young girl in wreath frame with garland and fleur-de-lis. Gold, enamel, and rose-cut diamonds. French. All courtesy of Fred Leighton.

Brooch by Serafini, Florence. Rutilated quartz and gold; circa 1965. Courtesy of Primavera Gallery New York.

FLORA

$\mathcal{P}$LANT life evokes perennial beauty. As a jewel, a leaf glittering in autumnal tones or a tanzanite window framing a moss agate gemstone are just some of the more lyrical brooches in this genre.

Tree brooch by James de Givenchy for Taffin. Mounted in gold and set with carved green tourmaline; 2003. Courtesy of James de Givenchy for Taffin.

Leaf pin by Vedura. Mounted in gold and set with precious and semiprecious gemstones; circa 1940. Courtesy of Newcal Galleries, Ltd.

"Plananal" brooch by Judy Geib.
Dendritic agate surrounded by
tanzanite, silver, and gold; 2006.
Courtesy of Judy Geib.

Consider two pins of a similar
theme or shape on a collar. Small
blossom branch pins by Ted
Muehling; 2007. Courtesy of
Ted Muehling.

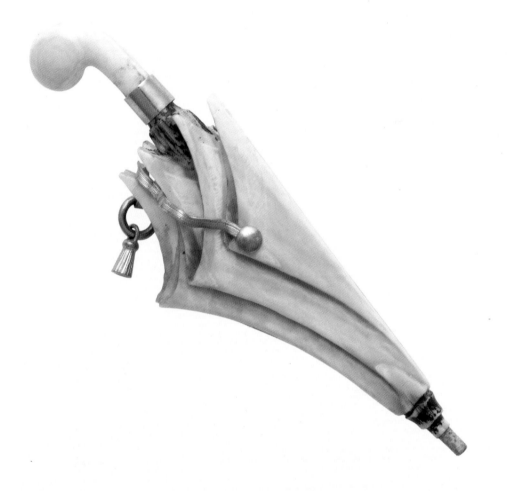

Victorian umbrella. Ivory and gold; circa 1880. Courtesy Kentshire Galleries, Ltd.

WHIMSY

*F*EEL free to amuse yourself and others because both the quirky and quaint hold court here. Umbrellas, dogs, cats, birds, and horn blowers—this is the pin as witty allegory. Whether fine or faux, these charismatic jewels should gratify your fancy.

Fantasy brooch by Chaumet, Paris. Mounted in gold and set with rubies, emeralds, and diamonds. Courtesy of Fred Leighton.

Shakudo is a Japanese alloy of gold and copper overlaid with gold and colored metals. This piece depicts a Samurai cat dancing to a rat playing the shamisen; circa 1850. Courtesy of Olivia Collings Antiques.

Made entirely of wire, this is a great costume piece for dog lovers. Collection of Gertrude Gramaglia.

"Chicken Little" by Donald
Claflin for Tiffany & Co. Mounted
in gold with enamel and set with
turquoise and diamonds; circa
1969. Courtesy of Smithwick
Dillion, Inc. NYC.

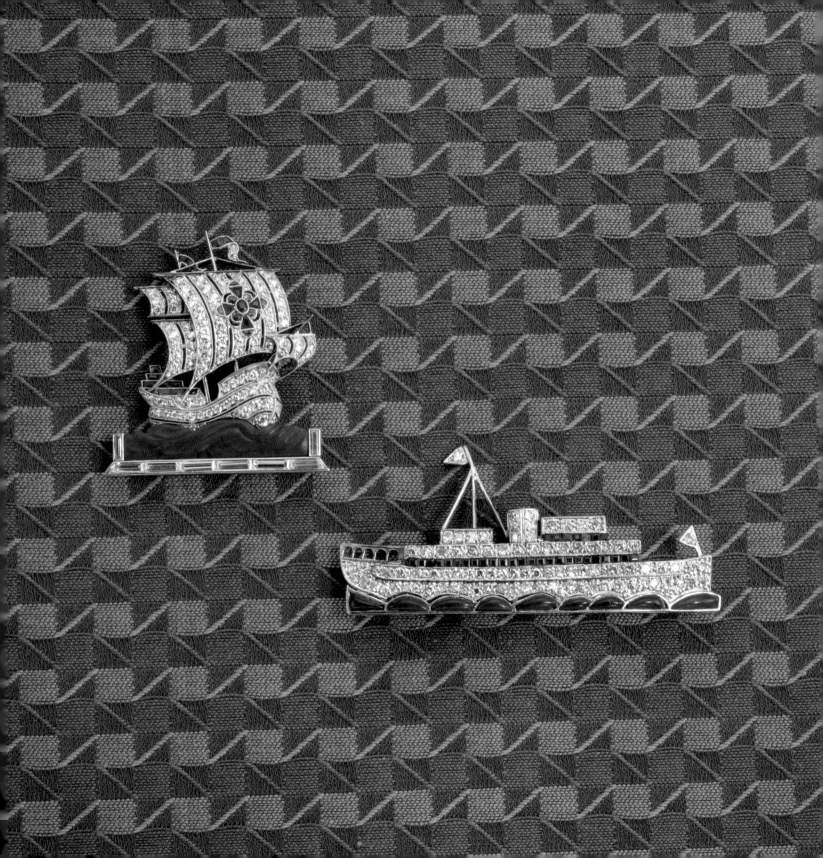

JOURNEY

A car, jeep, and ship are travel modes that take us near or far. In the form of delightful pins, these miniature representations elicit conversations recalling the early days of the automobile, luxurious cruises, and even wartime memories.

Sailing ships. Left: Platinum-mounted diamond and multi-gem-set brooch in the form of a tall ship sailing in lapis lazuli waters. J. E. Caldwell & Co., Philadelphia; circa 1930. Right: Platinum and diamond brooch, in the form of an ocean liner, set with calibre-cut sapphire windows and buff-cut lapis lazuli seas. Possibly by J. E. Caldwell & Co., Philadelphia, circa 1910. Courtesy of A La Vieille Russie.

Golden travels. Top: Jeweled antique car pin in gold. Bottom: "Three Men Riding in Willy's American Jeep." Mounted in gold and set with rubies, ruby beads, and sapphire bead; circa 1940. All courtesy of Fred Leighton.

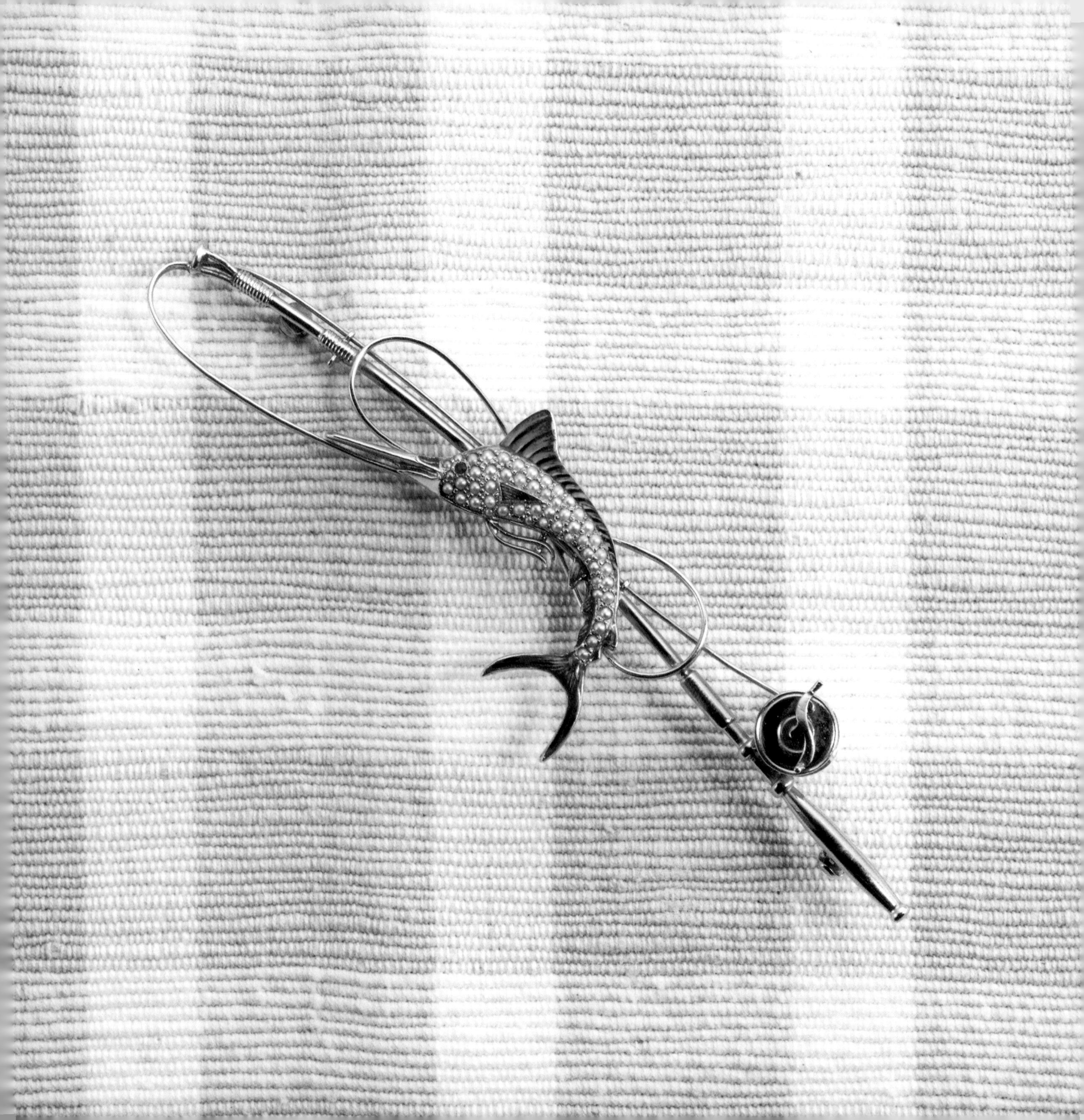

AQUATIC

Our fascination with the sea is eternal. Shells, ocean life, and even foamy waves serve as inspiration for brooches that stir the ancient mariner in all of us.

Blue marlin sport-fishing brooch, with rod and revolving reel. Gold, enamel, and seed pearls. American, circa 1940. Courtesy of A La Vieille Russie.

A sweet little fish enameled in white. Collection of Ellen Nidy.

"Breaking Wave with Seagull"
by Oscar Heyman & Brothers,
Inc. Mounted in gold and
platinum with enamel and set
with diamonds. This design was
first made in 1956. Courtesy of
Oscar Heyman & Brothers, Inc.

"The Ancient Mariner" by
Marilyn Cooperman. Mounted in
gold and patinated silver and set
with diamonds. The original
design for this brooch was
created in 1998. Courtesy of
Marilyn Cooperman.

Undersea brooch. Gold, enamel, diamond, and pearl; circa 1880–90. Private collection, courtesy of Williams Galleries, Nashville.

Mermaid pin. Gold, Baroque pearls, silver, and rose-cut diamonds. Table-cut diamond set in mirror; early nineteenth century. Courtesy of the DeYoung Collection.

The ocean's gift is transformed into sparkling adornment. Shell brooch by David Webb. Seashell mounted in gold and set with emeralds; circa 1955. Courtesy of Primavera Gallery New York.

Gold "Aureole" brooch by Judy Geib; 2004. Courtesy of Judy Geib.

Gold, diamond, and ruby pin by Andrew Grima; circa 1960. Courtesy of Primavera Gallery New York.

CURVILINEAR

FORM plays an important role in the attraction of a pin. Be it bold, lyrical, or brilliant, these shapes enliven the space they occupy on the garment.

Enamel landscape miniature.
Mounted in gold with
filigree frame. Courtesy of
Fred Leighton.

Gold circle of wheat pin by
Georg Jensen; circa 1957.
Courtesy of Smithwick Dillon,
Inc. NYC.

Vintage plastic yellow leaf. Collection of Deborah J. Gardner. Green strawberry pin by Joli.
Composite of vintage elements. Brooch by Michael Good.
Patinated bronze and gold; circa 2004. Both author's collection.

UNCONVENTIONAL MATERIALS

*P*APER or plastic? The use of unconventional materials in jewelry permits countless designs to be realized. Conventional rules are tossed aside in favor of originality. This freedom of expression leaves one to decide whether to wear a pin to the grocery store or out to dinner.

"Triple Poppy" brooch by Seaman Schepps. Hand-carved sandalwood, citrine, pearl, yellow sapphire, and gold. Photograph courtesy of Seaman Schepps.

Bakelite. Collection of Sandra Gilbert Freidus.

Flower brooch. Lucite; 2007.
Courtesy of Alexis Bittar.

"3D Block Origami" pins by
Masao Yamada. Clockwise
(from top left): "Hino-Tori" (fire
bird), "Hino-Tori," "Sunburst,"
"Sunburst," "Hino-Tori;" Center:
"Sunburst." Paper; 2007.
Courtesy of Masao Yamada.

Bead artist Karen Paust
creates lyrical brooches by
hand-working glass beads, nylon
thread, copper wire, and a
sterling silver pin back. "Suzen's
Hibiscus;" 2002. "Squash
Blossom;" 1997. Photographs
by T. E. Crowley. Courtesy of
Karen Paust.

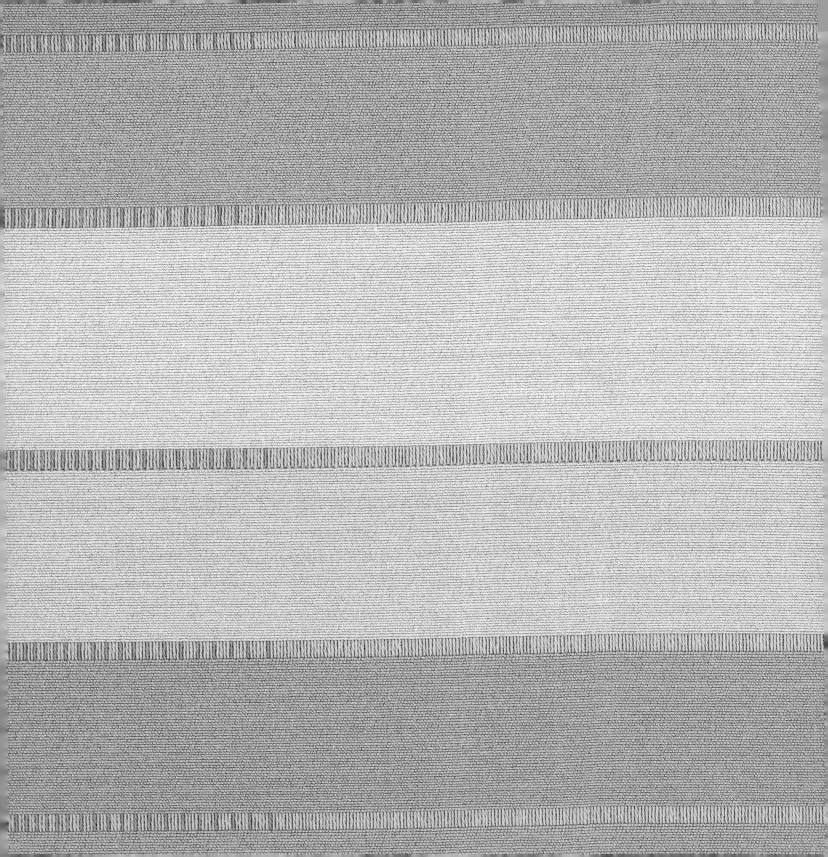

Chapter 6

CARE

*W*HEN purchasing jewelry, first consider whether the item suits your personal style and fits your budget. Then determine how this piece works into your present wardrobe. Ask yourself: When will I have an opportunity to wear it? Will I tire of it by the next season or by the following year? While shopping for pins and brooches, remember that the purchase should always be a joyful experience.

To ensure that your new acquisition will provide you with lasting pleasure, you must learn the hallmarks of fine craftsmanship. Never sacrifice quality for a bargain price because there is no substitute for a beautifully executed piece. In the long run, it is worth the investment to pay more for a pin that is discernibly better in quality.

Brilliant-colored gemstones enliven a soft and neutral jacket. Sarpech brooches by Munnu/The Gem Palace. Mounted in gold and set with multicolored spinel. Courtesy of Munnu/The Gem Palace.

Identifying an expertly crafted pin is accomplished by simply inspecting the ornament. Learning to use a jeweler's loupe is a good idea and a great way to view small details such as the gold work, catch, or the joint of a pin stem. When you look through a loupe, you will see exactly how the piece was made. First, check the reverse side. The back of a well-made piece of jewelry should be finished as nicely as the front. Take a look at how the metal is worked. Is it wonderfully shiny and smooth or does it have an uneven, rutted surface with clumps of metal here and there? Are all the surfaces polished to a high shine? Does the entire pin feel smooth when you run your hand over the piece? There should not be any sharp edges.

Check the pin clasp to be sure it works properly. Most modern and contemporary pin backs are made of the same metal as the rest of the piece, but a vintage clip may have a replacement. If this repair has been done well, the work will look seamless; replaced parts should be clearly pointed out to you by the individual offering it for sale.

The network of openings that hold the gems in place is called *ajoure* work. When viewing them on the reverse side of the pin, these apertures will have a high polish so that the reflection off the metal will bounce back into the stones, allowing them to sparkle more brightly. Gems should never be glued into a mounting and the retailer should know their type and grade; they must also be of a quality that corresponds to the level of workmanship and overall cost of the ornament. Answers to your questions should give you more confidence about the jewel. This last

point is essential. As the consumer, it is your responsibility to ask any reasonable question concerning your intended purchase. Anyone who dismisses your inquiry or makes you feel uncomfortable is not the right retailer for you. A salesperson should be courteous and professional.

As for size, bigger isn't always better quality-wise. Smaller, beautifully crafted pieces can have a significant impact, especially when worn in combination with other pins. Even when worn alone, a truly exceptional but modest-sized pin will hold its own. Vintage pieces usually have this kind of appeal, and the quality of what you will find is often quite lovely.

STORAGE AND REPAIR

Whether it is a piece of fine or costume jewelry, keeping a pin in prime condition maintains its beauty and value. Always store a pin in its original case or box, if you have it. Zippered poly bags are inexpensive and can be purchased in office supply or craft stores. They are the perfect thickness and size for most brooches; the fact that they are transparent helps when trying to choose one to wear. Elaine Mack keeps her pins in her closet on flat velvet pads that she buys at a jewelry supplier. When she is getting dressed in the morning she simply pulls out the pad, selects the pin she wants

"Shooting Stars" brooch by David C. Freda. Fine silver, 14-, 18-, and 24-karat gold, enamel, and freshwater pearls; 2003. Photograph by Ralph Gabriner. Private collection of Camilla Dietz Bergeron, Ltd.

to wear, and attaches it. Another stylist I know takes the same pads and wraps each one in tissue. Then she slides them into a chest of drawers, one on top of the other. Whatever system works for you, the primary objective is to keep each pin in its own protected space. A scratched, dinged, or damaged brooch just isn't as attractive as it would be with very basic care.

Maintaining your pins with occasional but careful cleaning or repair is essential. If the piece is gem intensive, it is important to have a jeweler periodically inspect the prongs that surround the gems to make sure their strength has not been compromised over time.

Seek out professional advice. There are some criteria to keep in mind when choosing a skilled craftsperson to repair or restore a piece. Ask these questions before you place your prized possession in his or her hands:

- Where did you train, and for how long?
- Exactly what will the job entail?
- How will the work be accomplished?
- How long will the repair take to complete?
- What is the cost?

A skilled repairer must explain to you all of the existing damage prior to taking on the job. He should explain all options available to do the job completely and professionally. If the jewel is vintage or antique, any precautions or limitations to performing the service requested should be explained to you. Never leave your jewelry for repair or restoration with anyone you do not have confidence

Bird and crescent pin. Mounted in silver-topped-gold and set with diamonds, rubies, and sapphires; circa 1890. Courtesy of Frances Klein.

Ribbon basket brooch. Mounted in platinum-topped-gold and diamonds, rubies, natural pearls, a sapphire, and an emerald; circa 1900. Courtesy of Frances Klein.

Diamond and natural Burma ruby clips (here attached to form a single brooch); circa 1925. Courtesy of Frances Klein.

in. If there is any doubt in your mind, get a second opinion from another jeweler.

A good repair or restoration is nearly undetectable. Period jewelry should not be over-worked or made to look brand-new. Jewelers vary in opinion when it comes to cleaning pins. Some recommend the use of an ultrasonic cleaner; others do not because it can detach loose-fitting gems from their settings and cause other damage. Cameos should not be put into an ultrasonic cleaner because the vibrations from the unit can cause the shell or gem to suffer further damage if the cameo is already cracked.

The way to clean a pin depends largely on the materials from which it was made. Georgian and Victorian closed-back settings cannot be submerged in water, since the moisture will permanently damage the foil that was originally placed in the back of the gems to enhance their brilliance. If this happens, the stones darken. The gentlest way to clean a brooch is to use a slightly damp, lint-free cloth. Just wipe down the jewel and pat it dry. A professional cleaning must be left to a trusted jeweler who understands the delicacy of estate pieces.

Certain repairs are important while others can devalue a jewel. If the catch on a pin is no longer secure, have a jeweler advise you as to what can be done to bring it back to working condition. Many old pins have a long pin stem that protrudes further than the ornament. This was a safety device. That extra bit of pin stem was meant to be threaded into the fabric to which the brooch is attached. Cutting down the pin stem will severely

Floral circle pin. Mounted in platinum-topped-gold and set with demantoid (green) garnets, rubies and natural pearls; circa 1905. Courtesy of Frances Klein.

Penannular (open ring) brooch. Mounted in platinum-topped-gold and set with diamonds and demantoid (green) garnets; circa 1910. Courtesy of Frances Klein.

reduce the value of the antique. The worst type of repair is done with lead solder, which can ruin a jewel completely. A lead-solder repair is nearly impossible to reverse because it becomes inextricably fused to the precious metal it is intended to mend. This type of repair is often permanent; later, should you wish to attempt a reversal, it is very expensive. Today's welding repairs are good for smaller tasks and are reasonably priced. However, the newest technology being used in metalsmithing is laser repair. Although this is costly, it is a virtually seamless form of restoration and a wonderful solution for valuable pieces that have been damaged.

USEFUL ADVICE FOR GETTING ALL PINNED UP

When attaching a brooch, lay the garment to which it will be affixed on a flat surface and then clip it on. This enables you to determine the brooch's position easily, and you can play a little with the piece to find the best location. Additionally, the tines of the pin can be put precisely through the fabric so that you do not break the threads. Always use the safety catch if there is one. Some of my friends in the jewelry field recommend using a stickpin tip, which is a bullet-shaped device that can be placed at the end of a pin for added security. If the tines leave holes, gently nudge the weave back into place with a fingernail, which will restore the yarns to their original place.

"Asphodele" clip by Van Cleef & Arpels. White and gray pearls mounted in white gold and set with diamonds. Photograph courtesy of Van Cleef & Arpels.

Pins and brooches are appropriate for any occasion. Throw one or more multi-hued and gem-laden beauties on a cocktail dress and watch the sparks fly. Top: Seaman Schepps "Fantasy" brooch, set with citrines, sapphires, diamonds, and a South Sea pearl. Bottom (left): Martin Margiela craft brooch; (right): Erickson Beamon antiqued crystal and gold brooch. Photograph by Raymond Meier.

ADDRESSES

A La Vieille Russie
781 Fifth Avenue
New York, New York 10022
212.752.1727
www.alvr.com

Bergdorf Goodman
Elaine Mack
Head Personal Shopper
754 Fifth Avenue
New York, New York 10091-2581
212.753.7300

Camilla Dietz Bergeron, Ltd.
818 Madison Avenue
New York, New York 10021
212.794.9100
www.cdbltd.com

Alexis Bittar
718.422.7580
www.alexisbittar.com

Chopard
709 Madison Avenue
New York, New York 10065
www.chopard.com

Christie's
20 Rockefeller Plaza
New York, New York 10020
212.636.2000
www.christies.com

Olivia Collings Antiques
oliviacollings@aol.com
www.oliviacollingsantiques.com

Marilyn Cooperman
212.921.2668
mfcoop146@gmail.com

The DeYoung Collection
608 Fifth Avenue
New York, New York 10020
212.541.7202
alan@thedeyoungcollection.com

Drucker Antiques
487 East Main Street, Suite 197
Mount Kisco, New York 10549

Tony Duquette Inc.
Beverly Hills, California
310.271.4688
hutton@tonyduquette.com
www.tonyduquette.com

Aaron Faber Gallery
666 Fifth Avenue
New York, New York 10103
212.586.8411
www.aaronfaber.com

Four Seasons Design Group
(Silver Seasons)
2400 Merrick Road
Bellmore, New York 11710
516.781.3155
www.fourseasonsdesign
group.com

David C. Freda
www.davidfreda.com

Garrard
24 Albemarle Street
London W1S4HT England
www.garrard.com

Judy Geib
718.599.5520
www.judygeibplusalpha.com

Michael Good Designs, Inc.
P.O. Box 788
Rockport, Maine 04856
800.422.9623
www.michaelgood.com

Hamshere Gallery
P.O. Box 3.0123
London SW13 0WJ England
www.hamsheregallery.com

Oscar Heyman & Brothers, Inc.
New York, New York
www.oscarheyman.com

Joli Jewelry
by Jody Lyons
117 Sterling Place, #15
Brooklyn, New York 11217
718.399.9150
www.jolijewelry.com

Joolbait Jewels
Julie Levine
www.joolbait.com

Kentshire Galleries, Ltd.
700 Madison Avenue
New York, New York 10021
212.421.1100
www.kentshire.com

Frances Klein
9470 Brighton Way
Beverly Hills, California 90210
310.273.0155
www.francesklein.com

Lalique
712 Madison Avenue
New York, New York 10065
800.214.2738
www.lalique.com

Lang Antiques
323 Sutter Street
San Francisco, California 94108
415.982.2213
www.langantiques.com

Fred Leighton
773 Madison Avenue
New York, New York 10065
212.288.1872

Joanne Lyman
163 East 81st Street, #9B
New York, New York 10028

Francis Mertens
Vesting Straat 59-63
Antwerp, Belgium
32.475.457.956

The Metropolitan Museum of Art
1000 Fifth Avenue
New York, New York 10028
www.metmuseum.org

Mish New York
31 East 70th Street
New York, New York 10021
212.734.3500
www.mishnewyork.com

Linda Morgan Antiques
lindamorgan@earthlink.net

Ted Muehling
27 Howard Street
New York, New York 10013
212.431.3825
www.tedmuehling.com

Munnu/The Gem Palace
49 East 74th Street
New York, New York 10021

Newcal Galleries, Ltd.
905 Fifth Avenue
New York, New York 10021

Old World Weavers/Stark Fabrics
The D & D Building
979 Third Avenue, 10th floor
New York, New York 10022
212.752.9000
www.old-world-weavers.com

Karen Paust
www.karenpaust.com

Primavera Gallery New York
210 11th Avenue, Suite 800
New York, New York 10001
212.924.6600
www.primaveragallery.com

Quadrille
Wallpapers and Fabrics, Inc.,
China Seas, and Quadrille Couture
The D & D Building
979 Third Avenue, Suite 1415
New York, New York 10022
212.753.2995
www.quadrillefabrics.com

The RSL Collection
New York, New York
suzylev@aol.com
robbisav@aol.com

Joan Rivers
joanrivers.com

James Robinson, Inc.
480 Park Avenue
New York, New York 10022
212.752.6166
www.jrobinson.com

Susanne Rubel
G. Torroni S.A.
Geneva, Switzerland

Seaman Schepps
485 Park Avenue
New York, New York 10022
212.753.9520
www.seamanschepps.com

S. J. Shrubsole
104 East 57th Street
New York, New York 10022
212.753.920
www.shrubsole.com

Siegelson, New York
589 Fifth Avenue, Suite 1501
New York, New York 10017
212.832.2666
www.siegelson.com

Gary L. Smith
Master Gemologist/Appraiser
pagemlab@comcast.net

Smithwick Dillon, Inc.
at Bergdorf Goodman
754 Fifth Avenue
New York, New York 10091-2581

Sotheby's
1334 York Avenue
New York, New York 10021
www.sothebys.com

Taffin by James de Givenchy
212.421.6222
www.taffin.com

Van Cleef & Arpels
744 Fifth Avenue
New York, New York 10019
212.644.9500
www.vancleef-arpels.com

Williams Galleries
4119 Hillsboro Road
Nashville, Tennessee 37215
615.297.2547
wmsamart@aol.com

Harry Winston
718 Fifth Avenue
New York, New York 10019
212.245.2000
www.harrywinston.com

Masao Yamada
PMB 230
6252 Commercial Way
Weeki Wachee, Florida 34613
352.596.1398
myamada@bellsouth.net

ACKNOWLEDGMENTS

Jewelry has always been and will continue to be an integral part of style. It was important to me that this perspective be felt throughout my book. If I have succeeded, it is largely due to the jewelers and private collectors who generously contributed their good will, images, and brooches. Their enthusiasm bolstered my desire to produce something that would serve as both a fashion guide and practical reference. Without their support, this would not have been possible.

Of course, this publication was made complete by the original photography of the brilliant David Behl. I knew of David's work, and was beyond thrilled when he agreed to join me in this venture. His validation of my neophyte ideas made what might have been an otherwise challenging experience, enormously fun and creative.

In addition, I must express my sincerest gratitude to everyone at Rizzoli, who not only welcomed my vision, but also worked with every intention of making it a reality. The prodigious efforts of my editor, Sandy Gilbert, must be acknowledged with unmitigated appreciation. Undaunted by piles of copy and photographs, Sandy got straight to work and created something incredibly organized and beautiful out of what seemed to me, sheer chaos. The design efforts of Miko McGinty, Doug Clouse, and Rita Jules are to be applauded not only for their expertise, but also for their sensitivity to the subject matter. I must also thank Pam Sommers for her stylist's eye and lending her fabulous collection of silver pins. Ellen Nidy was instrumental in her guidance, and showed her "pin spirit" by allowing us to photograph an ornament from her own jewelry box. Many thanks to Linda Pricci's aunt, Cathie Klitin, who kindly allowed us to photograph a precious family heirloom. A big shout out goes to Henry Casey and Walter de la Vega, without whom a tiff file would never have been opened or analyzed correctly. Thanks to Maria Pia Gramaglia, who also lent us jewelry, and Kaija Markoe for their care in the production of book.

I am most grateful for the wonderful words of Dame Elizabeth Taylor, a pin collector nonpareil. Jewelry is nothing without context and the wonderful story of her Schlumberger brooch adds yet another facet to this ornament's legendary narrative. I must